Advanced Principles in Teaching Classical Ballet

UNIVERSITY PRESS OF FLORIDA
Florida A&M University, Tallahassee
Florida Atlantic University, Boca Raton
Florida Gulf Coast University, Ft. Myers
Florida International University, Miami
Florida State University, Tallahassee
New College of Florida, Sarasota
University of Central Florida, Orlando
University of Florida, Gainesville
University of North Florida, Jacksonville
University of South Florida, Tampa
University of West Florida, Pensacola

University Press of Florida

Gainesville

Tallahassee

Tampa

Boca Raton

Pensacola

Orlando

Miami

Jacksonville

Ft. Myers

Sarasota

John White

Advanced Principles in Teaching Classical Ballet

Library of Congress Cataloging-in-Publication Data
White, John, 1934 Dec. 9–
Advanced principles in teaching classical ballet/
John White.
p. cm.
Includes bibliographical references.
ISBN 978-0-8130-3297-9 (alk. paper)
1. Ballet—Study and teaching. 2. Ballet dancing.
I. Title.
GV1788.5.W475 2009
792.8079–dc22   2008025851

The University Press of Florida is the scholarly
publishing agency for the State University System
of Florida, comprising Florida A&M University,
Florida Atlantic University, Florida Gulf Coast
University, Florida International University,
Florida State University, New College of Florida,
University of Central Florida, University of
Florida, University of North Florida, University
of South Florida, and University of West Florida.

University Press of Florida
15 Northwest 15th Street
Gainesville, FL 32611–2079
http://www.upf.com

Dancers are the athletes of God.

Albert Einstein

Artist's Pledge

Experiencing art allows one to find perfection in an imperfect world. However, mistaken beliefs hold tenaciously on to false precepts that would cloud perceptions and inhibit the creation of beauty. In the end, truth will win the day *if* it is vigorously sought after. Students of the arts must refuse arrogance and self-righteousness, which have no place in the pursuit of excellence.

It requires real courage to confront what is erroneous and proclaim the right way. Truth enlightens understanding. And this illumination is reflected in the good works of adherents who have the power to change the universe. Only in this way will chaos change into order. Therefore, let there be light!

Contents

Preface

Advanced Principles in Teaching Classical Ballet is a sequel to my 1996 book, *Teaching Classical Ballet*, which provided elementary guidelines for serious ballet teachers. *Advanced Principles* covers advanced technical issues as well as addressing the current state of affairs in classical ballet and the art's future.

Specific teaching issues are presented here, including essentials on turning, jumping, and balancing. I outline a class construction format for intermediate and advanced students. I also discuss aspects of partnering, pantomime, and musicality, the value of rules, the discipline of learning, and the importance of the mental side to studying dance.

I base my methods on the those of the great Russian teacher Agrippina Vaganova. This book ends with a brief account of her career with the Imperial Ballet (later the Kirov Ballet) of the Maryinsky Theater in St. Petersburg. I would also recommend Vera Krasovskaya's biography, *Vaganova: A Dance Journey from Petersburg to Leningrad*, which the University Press of Florida published in 2005.

Finally, as in my first book, this work ends with more "Bits and Pieces," tidbits of significant information including reminders that help us all stay on the straight and narrow pathway to excellence.

Although I never had the privilege of meeting Agrippina Vaganova, I feel that I know her. I have dedicated my life to the study and application of her invaluable teaching principles, which came into my life through Victor Zaplin, my teacher and mentor. Zaplin was a Bolshoi Ballet Company ballet master who was sent to Cuba to teach and coach and to help establish the Cuban National Ballet School. These events occurred during my years as a member of the Ballet Nacional de Cuba (1960–64).

I wish to express special appreciation to Fernando Alonso, who was the artistic director during my years as a member of the Ballet Nacional. I have never before or since worked with such a dedicated and knowledgeable artistic director. The enormous successes of the Cuban company and Cuban dancers today are largely due to Alonso's leadership during the company's formative years. It was a privilege for me to be part of that effort, and I will be forever grateful for the opportunity.

More than seventy of my students have gone on to professional careers throughout the world as dancers, choreographers, ballet masters, and teachers. In addition, I have taught nearly eight hundred novice and experienced teachers who have attended my seminars eager to learn the teaching method named after Vaganova. In his own way, each has felt the guiding philosophy of Vaganova's methodology. I am proud of their achievements and desire to be part of her legacy.

Introduction

*A great teacher such as Jascha Heifetz helps you
capture the ecstasy, not the craft. "Touch my heart,"
he used to tell his students. "Make me cry."*

Paul Rosenthal

Knowledge is power. Therefore, as in all human endeavors, extraordinary effort fortified with comprehensive understanding has a great advantage over attempts to succeed based on deficient information or cursory preparation. Why then is there so much ignorance in areas of specialized study that require a profound comprehension of how to use tools to achieve desired results? Ignorance in classical ballet education seems to be impacted today by an impatient rush toward mediocrity. Curing this problem will require a multifaceted frontal attack involving every serious ballet professional, especially teachers. Let us dedicate ourselves to remedy this problem by acknowledging past mistakes and searching for solutions.

Classical ballet is a theater art normally performed before a viewing audience that comes to be inspired and thrilled by their experience. In this regard, dancing differs from painting or poetry, which are used primarily to express individual impressions. The object of art should be to create images that affect the beholders' perceptions. Another aim should be to awaken dormant understanding and reflect on the myriad possibilities of beauty. Art is not just an isolated object of creativity. Musicians, singers, and orators can hear the result of their own creativity. In this sense, they tend to be their own harshest critics. But dancers cannot see their own dancing. They must depend on viewers to corroborate that their efforts are worthy.

Dancers do not go home alone, lock the door, turn on the music, and dance *Swan Lake* around the furniture. As a theater art, dance needs an audience, and artists who engage in it experience a profound satisfaction from a job well done. All performing artists and their appreciative audiences share this experience. They need each other. At the same time, dance is a fleeting art. Each performance is unique unto itself. Artistic triumphs attained during one performance cannot be carried over into another. Dancers begin anew every time they step out onto the stage in hopes of enticing acclaim from a fresh audience.

Theater audiences are multifaceted. One sees fur-draped and bejeweled society matrons on the arms of tuxedoed escorts proudly taking their seats in parquet circle boxes. Many are dedicated supporters of the arts who are needed to help fund worthy projects. Other attendees include casual first-timers who, for various reasons, decide to give ballet a try. There are also those who have been reluctantly but dutifully dragged along by spouses or friends. In addition, one can see in attendance families of budding aspirants who recognize the value of "continuing education" for their children.

And there are the ever-present balletomanes, ballet lovers, well versed in the intricacies of the art with a broader horizon of appreciation. Balletomanes attend every performance, travel to faraway dance venues to see visiting companies, watch videos, read reviews, and know the reputations of many of the dancers. We in the business are grateful for each and every one who supports our art by gracing our performances.

Regardless of their motivations, all classical ballet audiences pay a fee to experience the vivid expression of intangible artistic talents. They are willing to do this because they lack the requisite talent to experience the art for themselves. Therefore, they have a right to expect the utmost proficiency in both technical virtuosity and artistic eloquence from the performers. Mediocrity has no place on any stage. Even unsophisticated viewers will leave the theater after a final curtain feeling unsatisfied if they have to sit through a poorly danced performance. They might not be able to put their finger on the precise reasons for feeling unfulfilled, but a weak performance will register as lackluster, and it will be much more difficult to coax them back into the theater to try again.

No one ever gets bored seeing a true artist perform a great masterwork. These are always memorable occasions that take on a life of their own in memory. Nevertheless, we are experiencing much mediocrity in the dance arts today. Can it be that, of all the theater arts, dance is the most subjective and therefore requires the most clarity to be fully appreciated?

It is not enough for a night at the ballet to be described as "interesting," which is a vague response to a performance that might also be interpreted as "different," "unusual," even "clever." Such diversions can be somewhat satisfying. However, a curious thing happens when one is exposed to a steady diet of "interesting" pieces to the exclusion of proven masterworks. One gradually becomes inured to lower expectations, so that even small improvements become "more interesting" and thus attract more attention.

Theater arts depend on knowledgeable viewers to appreciate and judge the quality of performances. For example, if music is not played well at an orchestra concert—if the conductor misinterprets the composer's intentions; if the musicians play wrong notes; if tempos are too slow or too fast—a well-tuned ear will detect the problem immediately. That is because dissonance is readily discernable.

Audiences notice when actors are miscast in a play, they forget their lines, or they fail to exhibit appropriate emotions. And the same criteria apply to grand opera. This is due to the fact that notes written in a musical score and words written in a script are essential reference tools that determine first-class performances.

Such is not the case in dance. Dancers are taught ballets, occasionally by the original choreographer, but more often by a ballet master who is charged with the task of remembering and rehearsing the piece. His or her memory can be fallible, and there is no guarantee that the ballet was learned correctly in the first place, especially when it is a third or fourth generation re-creation.

There have been attempts at rectifying the question of accurate restagings of ballets through written recording systems such as Labanotation. This helps to some extent. But written notes, regardless of how detailed, cannot provide many of the subtle nuances in dance movements that were intended by their creators, especially works created many years ago. Therefore, these recording systems have not been widely accepted.

For the most part, dancers who perform established works must rely on the memories of choreographers and ballet masters. It is known that the great choreographer Mikhail Fokine often forgot dance sequences in his own ballets and either changed steps or relied on the memories of past interpreters. Who can truthfully say that any company dances *Swan Lake* today exactly the way Petipa and Ivanov envisioned it in 1895? Even Tchaikovsky's clearly recorded music score for the ballet has been altered countless times.

Technology has facilitated the re-creation of previously choreographed ballets through videotapes, DVDs, and digital cameras. These aids help in re-staging and rehearsing, but they are only supportive guides for ballet masters and dancers. The most useful rehearsal aids are films of past performances, but even they are not necessarily accurate re-creations of the choreographer's original intent.

With regard to new choreographic projects, only the choreographer knows what he or she intends. What is seen onstage may or may not be that intention, once the responsibility for rehearsing passes to the hands of others, until ultimately the audience sees the performing artists' interpretations. If a movement seems awkward, did the choreographer intend the step to be done that way, or was it a faux pas on the part of the dancer? If a dancer's expression seems to be at odds with an emotion or mood being portrayed, is it a lapse by the performer, or could the choreographer have been playing with our feelings? If the dancer begins or ends steps out of the music, might this not have been the choreographer's design?

Such evaluations by viewers are made easier when watching performances of well-known classics because there is a basis for comparison. How many singers have interpreted the leading roles in *Aida, Rigoletto,* and *Eugene Onegin*? How many actors have performed in *Death of a Salesman* or *Uncle Vanya*? How many orchestras have performed Mozart and Beethoven symphonies? And how many ballerinas have portrayed Giselle, Swanilda, and Odette-Odile?

Pondering the accuracy of the physical senses in judging a performance leads us to agree that it is easier to fool the eye than the ear. The conclusion must therefore be that the ear may be a more sophisticated organ. How is this paradox to be resolved? The answer is to go to the theater often to see the best possible performances and performers. Do not support mediocrity, no matter how well disguised, unless it is honestly presented as a stepping-stone to future excellence (e.g., a work in progress or a workshop performance). Bring to the theater an expectancy of excellence. Demand it. And most important, compare performers who dance the same roles. Don't be satisfied to see a ballet just once. Also, give a disappointing performer a second chance to redeem him or herself. Sometimes mishaps undermine an otherwise good effort.

Quality performers and performances have their roots in the process of quality education. Although audiences do not particularly care about dancers' educations, the process of enrichment through quality theater arts is dependent on schooling and the enormous responsibility of teachers. Excellence on the ballet stage relies on the preparation that students receive during their formative years in school. The purpose of this book is to stimulate the quest for unqualified excellence and provide guidance on certain critical aspects of teaching classical ballet.

It is a daunting task for teachers to help hardworking students wend their way through the morass of challenges. While engaged in this process, contemplating the odds for achieving success might be discouraging. Statistics show that barely one student in a hundred has the potential to become a professional dance artist, and the odds are even greater for rising to the highest levels of artistry. There are so many variables, and all of the marbles have to be lined up just right. Ironically, the final hurdle has nothing to do with training or talent. In the end it is the ballet director's subjective opinion based on personal taste. (I was once eliminated at an audition before anyone had had a chance to dance a single step. The first cut excluded all dancers who did not have brown eyes. My eyes are green.)

The fact that this is a daunting uphill climb is not such a bad thing, because many former ballet students who abandon the battle, for whatever reason, often become the art's most ardent theatergoers and supporters. But this only happens as the result of an enjoyable student experience. As educated voyeurs, such former students are likely to be acutely interested in the offerings they view, due to their personal experience.

Ballet experiences for viewers at all levels should be magical and exciting, as performers strive to reveal choreographers' intentions. It is the responsibility of performers to project across the footlights and touch the emotions of viewers. Dancers should also perform in a skillful and enticing manner that captivates and elevates the audience from the mundane worlds they normally inhabit. Are all dancers, choreographers, and musicians capable of this transformation? Do they have the skills to raise aspirations and fulfill audience expectations? Answers to these questions ultimately determine the quality of performances.

Although the intricacies of art education per se do not interest most theatergoers, they are clearly an important part of the equation. And the responsibility for passing on the requisite skills to students rests on the shoulders of knowledgeable teachers. Unfortunately, mediocrity in the art of ballet pedagogy is just as prevalent as in other human endeavors. When teachers take the easy road or coast on their professional laurels, they do a disservice to young hopefuls who come to their classes with high expectations.

Without a doubt, the quest for excellence requires conquering many obstacles. It is hoped that this study will guide readers to higher levels of professionalism in teaching the art of classical ballet.

The discussions throughout this book require that readers be able to visualize what is being described via written words. This is not a coffee-table picture book. Therefore, in order to coax the essential ability of visualization out of readers, I have purposely avoided using photographs and illustrations, so common with most ballet books. Although at first glance it might seem easier to illustrate descriptions with photographs, it has been proven that mental visualization is an important aspect of focused learning, especially in pursuits where there is an essential mind/body connection. In addition, visualization obligates teachers to choose the right words to create accurate mental images, so that their students will be able to internalize explanations both mentally and ultimately physically. All good ballet teachers possess this communication talent.

Teachers who develop empathetic abilities generally have a clearer view of exactly what they want their students to do in every aspect of their dancing. It is a refined method of instruction that places an obligation on students to focus attention and concentrate intently on what their teachers are giving them. On the surface it would seem that teaching based primarily upon verbal instructions flies in the face of the commonly held cliché that "a picture speaks louder than a thousand words." And it goes without saying that ballet is a purely visual art from the perspective of the audience. However, the two-way communicative aspects of teaching and learning demand a level of conscientiousness from both teachers and students that ultimately separates determined learners from distracted fun-seekers.

The following pages discuss some critically important aspects of teaching classical ballet technique particularly dealing with placement, balance, equilibrium, jumping, and turning fundamentals. Other chapters that contain valuable information such as partnering and pantomime are also included. Finally, as in my previous book, readers will find at the end more "Bits and Pieces," which are meant to increase their stockpile of important "pearls" while also stimulating thought.

I fully understand that some of my observations might be construed as being controversial. I might even step on a few toes along the way. But I urge readers to attack these pages without preconceived notions that might inhibit the possible germination of new ideas. Everything stated herein is based upon a half century in the ballet business as a professional dancer, teacher, choreographer, company director, and writer. No opinion or guideline is recommended or factually stated that has not been proven. Also, readers may occasionally find the same or similar ideas stated more than once. This is not an oversight or forgetfulness on my part. Reiterations appear because of their importance. Pay special attention to them.

Although I am still actively teaching students in the classroom, my main work at the present is teaching teachers how to be better at their craft. This effort is done through seminars on the Vaganova syllabus that I give at least once a year. Through the years nearly eight hundred novice and experienced teachers have attended my courses. Attendees represent ballet companies, university dance programs, private schools, and other organizations from virtually every continent in the world. Many have reported remarkable results after applying the Vaganova method. It has produced many outstanding artists during the past eighty years and continues to do so.

As a former soloist, teacher, and ballet master of the Ballet Nacional de Cuba, I have been fortunate to work with some of the best teachers and dancers in the business, and I am grateful to each and every one of them for what they have taught me. And the process continues.

So much for this introduction. I hope that it has stimulated readers to continue probing for answers to perplexing problems that plague ballet pedagogy. In the following pages are to be found important in-depth analyses of some critical aspects of teaching classical ballet that began with my original book, *Teaching Classical Ballet*. What follows are more advanced principles.

CHAPTER I

The Teacher's Role in Classical Dance

*Teaching is more than just the giving of information.
Teaching is a total commitment in which we must
be involved not only in the classroom but in all
areas of student activity.*

Robert Mange

What are the "secrets" of teaching classical dance? Are there, in fact, any secrets? The purpose of this chapter is to clarify vague concepts, stimulate analysis, and arrive at a common understanding of teaching principles.

If it is the mission of every performer to demonstrate as clearly as possible technical dominion, choreographic content, and artistic sensitivity to their audiences, then why are these essential ingredients so often absent or at best obscure today? This lamentable fact induces many dance theatergoers to seek out more and more cutting-edge performances rather than suffer through poorly staged ballet classics. At least some of these contemporary works are testing new limits of technique and expression and show some originality.

Classical ballet is an art that has stood the test of time. Naysayers who lament the stodginess of classical dance would have us lay to rest the great masterpieces of the past. "We must keep up with the times," they say. But can one imagine a world of classical ballet without *Sleeping Beauty* or *Swan Lake*? And what about *Giselle* and the modern classic, *Romeo and Juliet*?

How long would a major symphony orchestra's music director survive if he excluded works by Beethoven, Mozart, or Bach from his repertoire? And what about the operatic stage without Puccini and Verdi? It's too absurd to seriously consider. Nevertheless, there are many who would relegate ballet classics to the scrap heap of passé forgettables—who claim that it is time to move on and bring the art up to date. This misguided notion betrays the fact that we have no creators making masterworks today.

What prompts this attitude? It is not because the great classics have become boring. It is because the ways they are being performed are not only boring but also inept. The solution is simple: hire excellent dance artists to perform good choreography at sensible prices. Even better: outstanding artists performing great choreography at reasonable prices will sell out the theater at every performance. (Read those last two sentences again before continuing. They are the key to raising classical ballet out of its doldrums.)

In a futile attempt to elevate classical ballet instruction to accommodate modern concepts of art and public taste, we are beginning to see a multitude of ballet teaching theories that can best be described as the Mish-Mash method. M&M involves a little of this and a little of that. It is a stew that attempts to circumvent proven methodologies in order to speed up the process. It emphasizes technical tricks to make the product (dancers) more exciting and marketable.

This innovative teaching approach is the product of uneducated teachers cherry-picking through established methods to formulate novel "best-of-the-best" systems. They borrow certain concepts of proven methodologies to form the basis of new or experimental ideas. Unfortunately, classical ballet is suffering because this state of affairs is receiving increasing impetus and approval, especially when advocated by the students of well-known M&M innovators. We are beginning to see students referring to their mentors' ideas as "methods," when in fact there never was a method, only a peculiar way of teaching. If the name is big enough, the "method" tends to be given credence by uninformed adherents.

Another unfortunate side effect of the M&M method has been a widespread explosion of the competition mentality. Instead of experiencing great art, we are now searching for "winners." Competitions focus interest on the emergence of new talent with the hope that the winners' infusion of new blood will somehow stir up public interest and make things better. But the opposite is taking place. Competitions are turning classical ballet into yet another spectacular dance-sport. Meanwhile, the current rage of competitions and dance conventions mainly benefits the pockets of presenters, venue locations, trophy and costume makers, choreographers, so-called master-teachers, and judges—with most of the expenses being underwritten by naïve parents. However, the art of classical ballet scarcely benefits, and there are unhappy consequences when losers must resign themselves to accepting "unfair" judgments.

Years ago, the original premise of international ballet competitions was based on discovering the epitome of the classical ballerina and premier danseur—i.e., the perfect Swan Queen and the ideal Albrecht. Keen interest was focused on talented emerging dancers. Nearly all of the prestigious medals were awarded to artists who epitomized these standards. It is thought-provoking that the majority of medals being awarded today in international competitions go to non-American dancers. Why? One of the purposes of this book is an attempt to answer this question.

In virtually every instance, dancers who have transcended the artistic and technical challenges of classical roles have realized that the art of ballet is revealed only through discipline and hard work. For true artists the work is not drudgery but a joyous endeavor in their pursuit of perfection.

A wise artist in any field realizes that perfection is not attainable, and one must not be obsessed with trying to achieve this impossible goal. However, to aspire to the highest levels of artistic achievement, one must continually work toward that end, knowing that there is always room for improvement, regardless of what audiences or critics say. Working at perfecting one's abilities, knowing that such a goal is unattainable, is not futile. It is the stimulus that ignites the passion to strive for ever higher objectives.

If one becomes complacent with plateaus of achievements attained, then one is doomed to wallow in mediocrity. And nothing is more deplorable in the arts than mediocrity in professional theaters, concert halls, and museums. Let such art lovers celebrate their interest and appreciation of the arts by becoming the arts' most ardent champions.

Lincoln Kirstein's contribution to classical ballet was invaluable as George Balanchine's devoted supporter. Wouldn't his role as benefactor have been greatly diminished if he had instead used his money and influence to try his own hand at choreography? The arts need champions like Mr. Kirstein. And there are worthy hopefuls who deserve the support of every dance lover, both on and off the stage.

This does not mean that only acknowledged geniuses should be allowed to study and perform. It just means that teachers must be completely honest with their students about their chances for becoming professional artists. Ballet classrooms are full of students who love to dance. Studying dance can be a rewarding experience, just like studying music, sculpture, or painting. There is no reason arts lovers should not study art. They need only to keep things in perspective when contemplating art as a profession.

Could a professional symphony orchestra survive if it employed musicians who had difficulty reading music, or who could not properly place their fingers on their violin strings, or who could not keep accurate tempo? Impossible! So why do we support so many small dance companies across this country who employ mediocre dancers?

The pursuit of perfection is always key to resolving this conundrum. But how can conscientious dancers, teachers, and choreographers discover the arduous pathway that leads to perfection? The answer is that it all starts with education.

Parents hand over their children to teachers who have the responsibility of providing the best possible education for their charges. If teachers are themselves ill prepared, then they are not equipped to handle that responsibility. This means that every teacher must learn how to teach. There is no other way. But it is not a self-study course. It can only be done under the tutelage of an acknowledged expert, one who has demonstrated that they have knowledge and expertise sufficient to help talented beginning ballet students become fully professional dance artists.

Unfortunately, such expertise is in very short supply. And so we must tolerate a host of ill-prepared teacher-wannabes who boast of expertise, but ... ? It's not that they do not care to learn pedagogy. The problem lies in the fact that they do not recognize their limitations and are unwilling to take steps to rectify the problem.

For those who would correct the situation, there is a test for recognizing such expertise. A good teacher demonstrates that he or she is consistently able to raise marginally gifted students to the level of professional competence. The fact is that it does not take a great deal of teaching skill to train a supremely talented student. It is the second echelon of dance students who rely on their teachers' skill and knowledge. It is this second echelon of well-trained students who is the resource pool needed by artistic directors of most professional ballet companies. The better prepared the students are, the more likely it is that they will find work, even pursuing significant careers beyond the corps de ballet level as soloists and sometimes as principal dancers in smaller companies.

Ballet teachers need to work within a proven syllabus of instruction principles. However, a syllabus is only an outline of the material to be covered—what, how, when. The teacher's experience and judgment fill in the blanks with artistic nuances and colorations required to create the complete text. This learning process helps students find their way up the steep climb to mastery of the technique and the art.

Every serious ballet teacher working at the professional level must be capable of preparing their students for the demands of ballet company directors and professional choreographers. They must learn their craft under a recognized expert. (I do not use the term *master,* as this implies a level of expertise far beyond that demonstrated by most of those who have anointed themselves with this unmerited title.)

Each teacher must decide which ballet methodology they prefer, as no one is able to gain complete expertise in them all. Each methodology requires a lifetime of study.

Teachers inevitably err when they attempt to inject the "best" of each method into what they then call their own system. This foolish attempt sits in judgment of proven methods—picking and choosing, like selecting cabbages in a supermarket. Instead, after deciding which method it is to be, it is most productive to accept the method's principles as absolute rules. Learn the whys and wherefores. Dig. Try to determine why a step is done a certain way and why other ways won't do.

Most proven methodologies do not accept the often quoted premise that there are many ways to perform a particular step or exercise and that all are equally valid. In fact, nearly all proven systems state emphatically that their way works the best, and "here is the reason why." It is usually best to defer to the chosen system's fundamentals and methodology. Do not protest that once upon a time you learned things differently from a teacher you admired and respected. Accept the new information as infallible. Find out "why" as you dig deeper. There is almost always a reason lurking somewhere. And, of course, if you are stumped in your own research and analysis, conscientious teachers will contact their mentor to get answers to perplexing problems.

This is especially important when an astute student asks you a question that you cannot readily answer. Never improvise an answer to get yourself off the hook. If you are unsure, tell the student that you will research the question and give them an answer as soon as possible. Then do your homework! Again, your teacher-mentor should be able to answer puzzlers that are not easily resolved.

Always prepare your lessons. In the beginning this may require hours of preparation. In due course, if you have been conscientious, the prep time will gradually shorten. Every lesson should revolve around a theme or leitmotif for the day, often determined by the requirements of the lesson's grand allegro or a new allegro step to be introduced.

You must also have a goal for the year, including a monthly plan and a weekly plan. Write out your plans—the more detailed the better—so that you can refer to them regularly. And make sure that you evaluate your students (and yourself) at the end of the year to determine if you achieved your goal. Be honest in your evaluation. You might discover that your expectations were too high or that personal lapses of boredom tempted you to advance your students at too fast a pace. Or perhaps, because you do not like to see your students struggle, you kept dishing out baby food.

During the beginning and intermediate years of study, slow music tempos are extremely important. Students at these levels are still thinking about what they are supposed to do. They are not yet able to combine complex choreographic demands and artistic nuances of steps in order to keep up with fast tempos. The mastery of quick petite allegro can be accomplished later in more advanced levels.

Constantly remind yourself that much of what you give your students is new information and needs time to be assimilated by them. You need to guard against rushing your students through material that seems relatively simple . . . to you. To them it may represent a daunting challenge. Be patient.

Develop the ability to empathize, to "get into the skin" of your students; to feel what they are experiencing. All good teachers have this ability. You will be able to help them through trouble spots more easily, and they will appreciate your ability to tell them exactly what they need in order to overcome the difficulty of the moment.

Resist the desire to dress up and dance for your students. This is especially tempting for new teachers recently retired from the stage. Although entertaining for the students (and maybe stimulating for you), it does not force the students to ponder their own dilemmas and perfect their own executions. The class you teach is not the place for you to impress or get into shape.

Learn how to describe *exactly* what the exercise is and how you want it done. Use only words—no showing, no practicing, no marking. Remember that one day (if you are still teaching) you will be sixty, seventy, or maybe eighty years old, and you will probably be doing much of your teaching in a comfortable chair.

Make sure that you observe every student in each class. Resist the temptation to focus on your favorites while ignoring the others. It may very well be that your favorite student is the one who disappoints you the most in the end. The conscientious struggler in the back row may be the one who pushes on and succeeds, and he or she will often be the most grateful for the special help you gave. Conscientiousness is extremely important. A focused and hardworking student can sometimes achieve heights beyond levels arrived at by talented but distracted students. Reward conscientiousness.

It is imperative to maintain a positive attitude in all aspects of teaching. Always come to your lessons with a genuine expectancy of making progress. See your students in a positive light. Do not look for defects and mistakes. Such an attitude tends to become self-fulfilling, and errors will inevitably abound. Avoid negative comments. Avoid destructive gossip. Never speak negatively with anyone about anyone else, no matter how serious the offense, except to make things right. Find something positive in every situation. Your life will be more joyful, and everyone will work harder to fulfill your positive expectations. The positive must always trump the negative.

And now for a radical change of subject that on first glance would seem to contradict what I just finished saying. Teachers must occasionally display anger or displeasure in the classroom. But such outbursts should be carefully orchestrated to attain a goal. They are premeditated pedagogic eruptions—precision rifle shots, not scattered shotgun blasts—designed to establish an important point. Such outbursts must never be based on ego or self-righteousness, and they must never be unreasonably directed. They are a teaching tool specifically designed to make an important point that indelibly remains in the minds of students.

Sometimes students must face reality. Either they are pulling up or they are not. Either they are turning out or they are not. Either they are pointing their feet or they are not. The "demons" of laziness—boredom, indecision, and lack of discipline—must always be controlled by the teacher. Otherwise, attention is not focused, and the opportunity to learn is lost. The teacher must always be in control.

Such examples of premeditated eruptions can take form in different ways. For example, after a poorly done exercise, the teacher can just lower his head and not utter a word for a longish moment. Then he can look up directly at the students and calmly ask them why they are not pulling up as instructed. Wait for an answer. Of course, there will be none. Then remind the students that they must apply to their exercises what they already know and that there is no excuse for not doing it. Then ask, "Do you understand?" Again, wait for an answer, but this time expect them to respond.

Another example: If students are bobbling a balance on demi-pointe after a pirouette while holding the barre, ask them why they are hopping or why they are lowering their supporting heel or their working foot to the floor. Then wait for an answer. Of course, there will be none. Then tell them emphatically, "Do not hop!" And have the students try it again. When they hop again (as they more than likely will), ask once again, even more emphatically, "Did you understand what I said before? (pause) Do not hop!"

When the movement is at last done correctly, remind everyone that overcoming such difficulties often is just a matter of deciding not to commit the error. They have to learn to be tough-minded.

Occasionally, teachers must deal with disrespect, when a student purposely ignores rules of decorum, etc. It is never appropriate to yell across the room at the wrongdoer. Instead, walk directly up to the student and stand "nose to nose" with him or her. Without being insulting, chew the student out in a firm and unemotional way. Then decide whether he or she should remain in the classroom or be asked to leave. Make it clear that the offender will not be welcomed back into the class without an apology. Make it clear that a repeat offense will warrant communication with parents. Follow through.

Students must learn that there are always consequences for decisions they make and actions they take, and they must face this reality. This is an important life lesson, and work in the theater is an act of life where discipline and conscientiousness are indispensable.

There are many other ways to command attention and resolve problems in the class. However, a wise teacher never lets the studio become too cozy.

When students can easily "read" their teacher, the teacher is in trouble. Students must always be kept guessing. They must wonder if the teacher is serious about what he is saying or if he is just kidding. This keeps them on the edge. There is an element of fear, but it is a special kind of fear that is rather benign. It has more to do with uncertainty. If students can figure out what makes the teacher tick, then they are more likely to try to take advantage of perceived weaknesses. Don't let that happen!

This does not mean that teachers should not be friendly. They should be equally affable with everyone. It is appropriate to show an interest in the lives of students, beyond what happens in the classroom. Inquire about students' other interests and activities. Attend an orchestra concert, school musical, or choral recital occasionally. Such support will earn respect and appreciation from both the students and their parents.

At some time during your teaching career, it will become clear that you should be thinking about how you can pass on the storehouse of knowledge that you have acquired (assuming that you have been conscientious in your endeavors) over your lifetime of study. If you are wise, you will require all of your assistant teachers to take the same teacher training course(s) that you did years before. If you are fortunate, it is possible that one of them may have demonstrated true pedagogic skills. Make sure that all of your teachers buy into the method that you espouse. Do not tolerate any differences of opinion. There must be total agreement if you want to achieve the best results.

It is natural that each teacher will develop his or her own teaching style. But the overriding methodology must be the same. Variety, in teaching classical dance, is definitely not "the spice of life." Differences among your staff's teaching methodology will only lead to confusion for your students, with the most persuasive teachers winning them over, even when not in the students' best interests. Be vigilant about this. It will save you much grief if you handle the situation sooner rather than later, even if it means letting a stubborn teacher go.

Succeeding generations of ballet teachers inherit the onus bequeathed to them by their mentors and past masters. Truly conscientious teachers who have dedicated themselves to meet this responsibility may discover new heights that offer a glimpse of perfection, far in the distance perhaps, but nevertheless evident. What a great and rewarding challenge!

CHAPTER 2

What Makes a Good Ballet Teacher?

*Never be intimidated by another's success. Because
someone's light shines more brightly than yours
does not mean that you must live in their shadow.
Discover, then radiate your own light.*

A. Sage

What makes a good ballet teacher? Such a simple yet profound question. On the surface the answer would seem obvious. But if you really ponder the query, you discover that there are many facets to the issue, therefore prompting many answers.

A first and obvious response is that a teacher must do no harm to his or her students. By "harm" I mean all aspects of endangerment, including physical and emotional abuses. This can never be tolerated.

Typical physical harm often stems from the teacher's perception that a student is lacking in one of the "essentials" of classical dance. A list of some of these physical insufficiencies would include turnout, extension, height, weight, general body size and shape, physical proportions, "pointability" of the foot, demi-plié, etc. It is vital that teachers understand that, while some of these physical requirements for classical ballet can be improved upon, most are gifts of birth. No amount of tugging and pulling and forcing will significantly bear fruit in the long run. And many regimens that attempt such improvement are dangerous, leading to long-term joint and muscle injury.

The remarkable genius of the great past ballet masters who devised the sequence of exercises in a well-ordered class is unquestioned. While some new theories have demonstrated long-term benefits, many other innovations have proven to be of little or no value. Even worse, some are detrimental. A series of exercises that comprise a balanced lesson designed to benefit students would seem an obvious requirement of good teaching. However, this approach is actually quite rare. Such an ambiguous state of affairs implies that there is far too much ignorance among teachers who have in their charge young students eager to learn. This situation imposes an onus on parents trying to find the best teacher for their children. The same also applies to adults who are searching out schools to attend themselves.

It is quite common to find teachers who are in the habit of overemphasizing one or more of the physical demands outlined above. Occasionally a teacher's emphasis might even achieve extraordinary results. But more often such results are temporary and at the expense of the student's long-term well-being.

A knowledgeable and well-trained teacher will be able to perceive each student's natural assets and also minimize their liabilities. If limitations predominate, then it is doubtful that the student has professional possibilities. Of course, he or she can continue to study dance for the love of it, but they must understand their limitations and study without unrealistic illusions about a professional career.

An emphasis on pushing a student's body beyond its natural capacities is the sign of a bad teacher. An even worse teacher is one who plays psychological games with their students. Young students' minds can be very vulnerable, especially in the hands of an unscrupulous and thoughtless teacher. Most teachers eventually learn that their students place them on pedestals and look up to them as mentors, sometimes even as parent substitutes.

Young students and especially older teenagers can be greatly influenced by male teachers. A wise male teacher will take extra precautions to maintain a proper arm's length, in spite of sometimes flirtatious girls trying out their wiles. The same applies to male teacher–boy-student relationships and even female teacher relationships with their students.

Unfortunately, there are examples of egoistic and self-centered teachers who have dug deeply mired pits that their students cannot climb out of. Imposing one's will to intimidate students is unforgivable. Potential artists run the risk of having their gifts permanently scarred beyond redemption, even in the hands of a sympathetic, wise teacher who might try to help them later on.

Every student comes to the study of ballet with preconceived notions of what it takes to become a dancer. Quite often these ideas are mistaken. It is the teacher's job to clarify and show the student that becoming a dancer is much more than a dream or a fantasy. It takes work—hours and hours of work, days and months of work, yes, even years of work. It can be tiresome and tedious at times, especially during the intermediate years of study, when students know what they are supposed to do but their bodies do not cooperate. Nevertheless, the work must be properly guided so that no time is wasted, either in having to unlearn incorrect information dispensed by a teacher through ignorance or malice or wasting valuable time in the hands of an intolerant or misguided teacher.

What can be reasonably expected of a good teacher? First, good teachers always come prepared for their classes. They spend sufficient time to prepare lessons appropriate for the class level using material learned through study with a knowledgeable pedagogue. The sequence of exercises, beginning with barre, into the center, adagio, and through the phases of allegro (petite, medium, and grand) is also the key to a well-thought-out lesson. And from day to day and month to month, the progression of lessons should lead to an overall goal for the year. The material given must always be age and gender appropriate. The comprehension of previously learned material by the student must also be taken in consideration. And a student's physical strength plays an important role.

Good teachers always arrive to class on time. It is irresponsible for teachers to be habitually late, and such a bad habit is a very poor example for teachers to give to their students. Teachers should plan their personal time so they never arrive late. If the students are expected to be on time—in uniform, hair combed, standing at the barre, and mentally ready to go—then it is reasonable for them to see their teachers as role models always beginning on time. It is important to remember that every valuable minute waiting to begin a lesson is a minute stolen from the students. And time lost in the beginning of a lesson always cuts into the study of allegro at the end. Such a bad habit results in lengthening the overall learning process.

Good teachers always make sure that, in a ninety-minute lesson, there are twenty minutes reserved for the allegro section. Since there is so much material to cover, the center and adagio sections of a lesson should take about forty minutes. This leaves thirty minutes for the barre (for intermediate and advanced students). Since the lesson begins with the barre, teachers must learn to apportion the proper amount of time for each section, beginning with the barre, so that there is ample time for allegro. If the time for the barre runs over thirty minutes, teachers must then make adjustments in the center-adagio portion, never in the allegro section.

Good teachers always make sure that the students have ample room to work at the barre. Classes must never be overcrowded. And after the students move into the center, they must be precisely placed in evenly spaced lines. It is best not to let students seek their own positions in line. Do not be predictable in this regard. Arrange the groups in random order, so that over time each student will stand in all areas of the room, including the spot directly in front of you. Keep lines straight and evenly spaced, with plenty of room between students. Rotate lines, so that all students have a chance to work in the front row. When giving corrections, look beyond the student standing right in front of you, all the way back to the farthest corner. Once again, do not be predictable!

Good teachers always give needed corrections to all students. It is tempting to focus attention on the best students. But good teachers search for ways to praise their less gifted students' "best" efforts as well. This means a lot to them. It will also oblige you to concentrate on each student's attempt at trying to make things work—for them.

Avoid always having the same, or the best, student demonstrate combinations. Spread the opportunities around. Sometimes the extra pressure of having to demonstrate makes a lazy or distracted student shape up. Even better, develop the skill of describing all essential technical and artistic aspects of your combinations verbally, aided by hand gestures. Practice this by imagining that you are confined to a wheelchair. Avoid the temptation to fully demonstrate your own combinations. Remember that, once you decide to leave the stage and are no longer under the scrutiny of a ballet master's eye, undesirable habits may infiltrate your repertory of movements and gestures. And students do not want to see their teacher struggle to move properly.

Good teachers never raise their voice in anger or frustration. Find another way to communicate. A loud voice may get someone's attention, but it also turns off the listener. Teachers must find a way to make learning an enjoyable experience. There is no question that learning to dance is work. But it must be a joyful endeavor that students (and you) should look forward to, not dread.

There are many examples of modestly talented students who have risen to great heights because their teachers helped them overcome seemingly insurmountable challenges. Unfortunately, there are also just as many gifted students who have been turned off by frustrated and poorly trained teachers.

Good teachers always remember that every student in the class deserves equal respect and attention, even the not so cooperative and lazy ones. Rather than giving up on them or making their lives miserable in your class, you must demonstrate that you are wiser than they are. Never let them see that they are upsetting you. Find a way to communicate and energize them. Do not give up this important task. You might be the only positive influence in their young lives, and you could make a huge difference, even if they eventually quit in frustration and never dance.

Students should never quit dancing because of a problem they have with you. Do not give them any such ammunition to complain about. See the good in them. If it is not obvious, then search for it. Also, make sure that a recalcitrant student's parent knows the facts and is not tempted to pay undue attention to exaggerations or false impressions passed along by the child.

Finally, be able to walk out of the studio and go on with your own life. Do not stew over problems that cannot be fixed before the next day or even those that are unfixable. Remember, dance alone is not life. It is something we elect to do to help us enjoy the life we make for ourselves. Bon voyage!

CHAPTER 3

Teachers and Master Teachers

*Development of technique means more than merely
increasing the quantity of entrechats, chaînés,
fouettés, pirouettes, and the like. Real technique
refers to how the dancer's body reflects the very
words of the language of dance.*

Vera Kostrovitskaya

Years of training as a student under the watchful eye of a knowledgeable teacher, professional company dance experience, even achieving recognition and fame—these have little to do with becoming a real teacher. I say "real teacher," because there are many who claim the title of "teacher" (even the highest honor of "master teacher") but in reality have little to offer in regard to the requisites of true pedagogy and are merely competent class-givers. What then differentiates a real teacher from a class-giver?

Genuine teachers are selfless individuals who not only possess a profound knowledge and training in their chosen field but also take time to develop the ability to communicate what they know to receptive minds, thus stimulating and encouraging their students to explore all possibilities. In classical dance, as in all arts, it is hoped that such receptive minds are also innately gifted in possessing the unique physical and intellectual attributes that are essential for success in this unique field. The three-part package of necessary equipment—body, mind, and conscientiousness—is a rare combination indeed. Nevertheless, it must be considered a prerequisite for life in the theater as a professional dancer. In addition, budding artists who choose to pursue this illusive goal need to demonstrate the potential for developing the refined sensitivities of musicality, emotional feeling, and myriad artistic qualities that are capable of revealing the beauty of classical ballet to viewers.

In reality, it does not take great teaching ability to give daily lessons to dancers whose professional skills are already formed. Not wanting to stray far from where the action is, such class-givers are often found in large urban dance centers. After retiring from the stage, they remain on the fringes of professional dance by giving lessons to their peers or to a younger generation of luminary hopefuls. Because of their past fame, many of these so-called master teachers sometimes attract large followings.

It is helpful if they have had a career on the stage. It is also helpful if they know a little about what they are saying, although profound knowledge is not a prerequisite to claiming the title. This is because "master teachers" sometimes advocate new theories of their own while ridiculing already proven ones. If they have a winning personality, their persuasive manner might convince even astute students and dancers. If they are successful in establishing a modicum of popularity, they will enjoy the adulation of novice students and the occasional accolade of professionals in the business. These are attractive and tempting reasons to pursue this avenue.

It is, however, incumbent on students and/or their parents to seek out teachers who demonstrate the ability to teach, not just give interesting lessons. The primary question students should always ask in evaluating potential teachers is, "Is there clear evidence of genuine teaching taking place in the classroom?" Meaning, is the teacher capable of guiding students from a place of not knowing to a clearer understanding of what is required in order to progress to higher levels of achievement? Of course, most novices and parents are unable to answer this critical question. Therefore, additional guidance is needed. It would be impossible to offer here an easy solution to this dilemma, except to say that finding the right teacher requires that parents and students should interview teachers who have attained a reputation for making real dancers out of the raw material that comes to them. Another helpful method would be to interview respected professional dancers who can offer thoughtful observations about their teachers.

In addition, there are other important questions that should be asked in helping to evaluate potential teachers:

1. How many students has the teacher trained from elementary level to professional status?
2. Are the teacher's lessons primarily maintenance classes designed to help already formed professional dancers keep in shape?
3. Can I really learn how to dance better in these classes?
4. Am I just being impressed by the famous dancers that I'm rubbing elbows with?
5. Am I becoming a better dancer because of these experiences? Or are the classes just entertaining diversions?

Honest answers to these questions will help guide wise seekers in their search to find teachers capable of helping them achieve desired goals.

I wish to make it clear that the title "master teacher" is a designation that few (if any) merit. It is certainly not a title that one has the right to award to himself. Throughout ballet history there have been many outstanding ballet teachers. However, bona fide master teachers can only be recognized by having mastered all of the requirements for leading elementary students to a level of professional readiness. And they are able to accomplish this remarkable achievement with a majority of their students, not only the most gifted. It is assumed, of course, that the students they have to work with possess the essential three-part package of body, mind, and conscientiousness. Using these criteria makes it difficult to award (or claim) the title of "Master." Therefore, it is wise to closely scrutinize anyone who dares to use this title.

There is another consideration in determining the credentials of a teacher. It is very unusual for teachers to teach students from their first lessons to graduation. In fact, after they have been in the game for a time, most teachers discover that they have an affinity to a certain age group of students. It is not unusual to relate better to one group than another, and it should be anticipated when evaluating teachers. Nevertheless, good teachers should not skip around from class to class or level to level. They understand the importance of consistency and continuity.

Successful results may be attainable from every imaginable type of teaching personality. This aspect of evaluating teachers is not so important, except to say that there should be a compatible personality matchup between student and teacher. Among teacher types there are the martinets (strict disciplinarians); there are the lovable grandmotherly types; there are the gregarious ones who like to talk; there are the quiet ones who require students to listen carefully in order to hear explanations and instructions; there are recent ex-dancers who like to demonstrate; there are senior ex-dancers who prefer to sit in their chairs when they teach; and there are teachers of every other imaginable persuasion. All varieties are potentially effective—if they know what they are doing. "The proof is in the pudding."

Committed teachers have two things in common. They never cease to learn. And they never become complacent with levels previously attained. If classes seem tedious, they find ways to raise themselves up out of the doldrums. For teachers dedicated to their work, challenges (together with concomitant rewards) abound in every dance lesson.

It is also incumbent on all teachers to prepare their lessons. Teachers who take time to be thoroughly prepared will more than likely be able to pass on their knowledge and insights. Conscientious novice teachers generally find that they spend a good deal of time in preparation. Often the time required to prepare a lesson is the equivalent of the lesson's time itself (ninety minutes of prep time for a ninety-minute lesson).

Teachers with many years of experience discover that they do not need to spend as much time preparing their lessons. For them, it may only be necessary to clearly think through the lesson's allegro theme for that day (assemblé, jeté, sissonne, batterie, etc.). It is a good guideline for teachers to plan their lesson around the grand allegro combination of the day or possibly a repeat of the previous day's combinations. Each conscientious teacher has his or her own method for preparing. Only incompetent teachers show up for class unprepared.

Except for classes for the most gifted students, every group is varied and diverse in ability and conscientiousness. How to reach the mind of each student is the teacher's challenge—often a very daunting one at that. However, even when working with "nondancers" (those without the necessary professional proclivities), conscientious teachers can help those students achieve a level above that which is easily attainable. It can be hard work. But becoming a good teacher requires much effort, just as it does to become a good dancer. And why not? Isn't that why we decide to commit ourselves to this great endeavor? Besides, no one ever told us that it would be easy.

Naturally, we would all love to take credit for developing a new Makarova or a Baryshnikov. But let's be realistic. This is unlikely to happen. If we are fortunate, we might have in our care a group of conscientious worker bees—possibly containing an occasional queen bee—and hopefully not too many drones. If we are knowledgeable and prepared in our work, even minimally talented students may be refined to professional caliber.

The sign of a real teacher is that he or she can take middling talent and, through hard work, help them to become useful dancers and achieve their dreams of dancing on the professional stage. Super talents don't require so much work. They rise naturally, just as cream does with milk.

However, on those days when we find ourselves teaching a group of mostly "drones," it is important to get a grip on our attitude and hoist ourselves up from the temptation to be bored or uninterested. It is much easier when we have in our class a group of dedicated worker bees. However, turning the daily grind into artistic endeavor is the real test of a good teacher. What follows is a secret on how to deal with the aforementioned problem. (But be sure not to tell anyone. It's just between us.)

If you arrive to teach feeling out of sorts, as soon as the lesson begins, make a concerted effort to focus acutely on how the drones are doing. Pick out one and find something to compliment about their effort. Give them a specific correction that will make their effort more likely to be fruitful. Then move on to another, and another, etc. Pretty soon you will find that your funky attitude is changing and that you are becoming engaged with the class. Then, believe it or not, you will inevitably discover that both you and the students are connecting. When the ordeal is over, you will find that the time spent was fruitful. The student(s) you helped will be grateful, and you will have enjoyed the time together. It works. Try it!

Make sure that you do not fill your schedule with many busy hours of just giving classes. This mistake will surely burn you out, and it is also boring for the students. Dedicated, focused teachers find that they have difficulty teaching more than two ninety-minute lessons a day. Of course, you can force yourself to do more if the money is good or if you own the school and have bills to pay. But, in this book, we are discussing how to be a "real" teacher. This means that the students should never suffer because you have problems to deal with.

Teaching a variety of classes may be diverting to some teachers, and it helps to avert boredom. However, students need to be in the hands of the same competent teacher over a period of time. This is the only way for teachers and students to bond and for the transfer of knowledge to pay dividends.

It is always best if the teacher is working for an organization that stresses the same instruction syllabus for the entire faculty. Otherwise, teachers will compete for the students' attention. The danger is that a less than competent teacher with little or no vocabulary might be able to garner the trust of a class of students based solely on an effusive personality, while a knowledgeable teacher could lose the trust of the students simply because he or she lacks a scintillating personality.

Students must never be thrust into the situation where they begin to compare their teachers or are tempted to judge the competence of their teachers or the value of the methods and material being espoused. Students should never have to choose between their teachers for any reason. This is another reason for teachers to keep the same class for a period of time. Three years is a good span. It gives teachers ample opportunity to get to know and reach their students.

Good teachers do not waste time in demonstrating every exercise during the lesson (except for beginner students who need extra care). Also, "marking" is unnecessary if the teacher is prepared and if the students are accustomed to hearing explicit verbal instructions that paint precise mental pictures. Teachers must develop an accurate and concise vocabulary that accomplishes this goal.

Some teachers are meticulous about using ballet jargon for each and every step, pose, position, direction, etc. While I applaud teachers who make this effort, I feel that it is unnecessary to be so dogmatic. It is okay to mix ballet terminology with ordinary language to describe a movement. For example, in describing a step one could say, "glissade en arrière" or simply "glissade backward."

I have found that students who are taught through strict adherence to French terminology are not particularly benefited by this language exercise. It is common throughout the world, even in the most prominent national ballet academies, to hear proper French terms mixed with the native language. Nevertheless, for those who prefer using ballet jargon, it is imperative that it be used correctly. Regardless of your choice, everyone should own and use Gail Grant's *Technical Manual and Dictionary of Classical Ballet*.

This little paperback is available from most booksellers. It will answer most terminology questions.

Never, never improvise an answer to a technical question posed to you by a student, or anyone else for that matter. If you are not sure of the answer, tell the questioner that you will research the issue and respond later. Then do your homework! Give the questioner the correct answer without delay—the next day if possible. It is always better to tell a questioner that you are not sure of the answer rather than to give an improvised response that might be wrong. Rather than being perceived to be fallible, you will exhibit a serious attitude that everyone can respect. You need to be foible-free in the eyes of your students. It would be disastrous if a wrong answer were to be discovered by a conscientious student who might possibly check up on you. Remember, teachers must never have feet of clay. They must always be poised on their pedestal above any hint of ignorance or impropriety.

Finally, your students are not *your* students. You have no claim on them, no matter how much time you have put in on their behalf. It is quite common for students, especially when they get to the upper intermediate or advanced levels, to wonder if there might be another teacher out there somewhere who can get them around a troublesome boulder-in-the-road obstacle. It is inevitable that, at some point in their studies, students will question why they seem to be unable to execute a particular turn, or jump, or whatever has been plaguing them. Since they believe that they are trying their best and doing what you tell them, it couldn't possibly be their fault. Of course not. Therefore, the only alternative is that it must be a shortcoming of their teacher.

So the day may arrive when certain students and/or their parents inform you that they have decided to change schools. The real reason(s) probably will not be expressed. It is usually the case that they have already begun to make arrangements for the change. This is often a difficult blow to accept, since you have generously given them your attention, maybe even a scholarship amounting to thousands of dollars. It feels like a betrayal. But you must let it go. Just drop it. No student is worth pining over, no matter how talented. If you are certain that you did everything possible to help, then the student is the ultimate loser. Maybe they will discover their error before it is too late.

Don't invest so much of yourself into your students that you have no life of your own. They deserve the very best instruction in the classroom and support outside the studio that you are capable of giving. However, when the school day has ended, learn how to leave the problems of the school behind you when you exit the building. Go home. Have a good meal. Watch a movie or your favorite sitcom. And get a good night's sleep. Not much will get done at 3 a.m.

CHAPTER 4   *The Application of Rules*

*People in the arts understand that knowledge and
wisdom come from the eye.*

Mary Alice White, Ph.D.

Good teachers understand that one of the most important aspects of the
daily lesson is to constantly challenge students to reach beyond the comfort
zone. In the beginning, everything an elementary student confronts is challenging and sometimes so daunting that it seems impossible to untutored
minds and bodies.

To help students overcome challenges, wise teachers give their students
rules to live by in the classroom. This means that nearly every new pose, position, and movement adheres to precise academic rules that guide students
through the process of learning new material. And since there are so many
technical ingredients to learn, rules help students keep their thoughts in order so that they can either expand their repertoire of new steps or simply
review previously learned steps with greater accuracy.

For the most part, many of these strange (and sometimes uncomfortable)
physical aspects of classical ballet training are not normal, especially in the
beginning. For example, ordinary citizens do not focus on precise alignment
when standing or walking or while engaged in their daily routines. Only certain specialized activities such as gymnastics, golf, or tennis demand levels of
precision beyond the norm. Therefore, perfecting new patterns of thinking
and moving is facilitated if students can fall back on rules to guide them
through the rigorous process. Once the rules are assimilated, they become

orderly subconscious guides that aid the application of new fundamentals and inevitable additional complications.

In the beginning, it is beneficial for teachers to explain the new material in detail and then remind their students of the rules that will guide them through the process, while insisting on a precise execution. Following this procedure creates guidelines that students can depend on for answers to their own questions or doubts. In the long run, by following this procedure, students learn to think their way through seemingly difficult challenges until they arrive at the point where they are able to do the movement without conscious analysis.

At first glance, it may seem easier for teachers to just show students what to do through demonstrations or verbal reminders. Indeed, most novice and unskilled teachers fall into this trap and demonstrate far too much. Demonstrating is a common teaching device, especially for retired dancers trying out their wings as new teachers. However, in the long run, it is imperative for students to internalize the essentials of everything they are learning through their minds into their bodies. The problem is that many teachers get tired of giving the same corrections over and over to uncaring students. After a while these teachers begin to overlook important fundamentals that are supposed to form a dependable foundation for the students. Such a lapse inevitably leads to overwhelming technical challenges for their students when demands become even more complex.

One recommended teaching device is to turn students' questions back to them by reminding them to follow the rule(s) that they previously learned. Such a tactic forces questioners to probe their own storehouse of knowledge, which in turn leads to higher levels of self-discovery. This method directs students to understand not only what they are supposed to do but also why they are doing something a particular way and no other. Utilizing this teaching tool may take extra time at first, until the students learn that they must exhaust their own resources before teachers answer their queries. In spite of the extra time needed to follow this procedure initially, it will ultimately speed up the learning process while building greater student self-confidence.

Assuming that the teacher is knowledgeable and has a thorough grasp of the requirements for teaching lessons appropriate for a particular class level, the teacher should ultimately be able to teach an entire advanced lesson with only verbal instructions—no time-consuming demonstrations, no "marking" with the music, and no long-winded explanations. This is the only way to achieve the desired goal of teaching an organized advanced ninety-minute lesson that consists of thirty-minute barre, forty-minute center, and twenty-minute allegro segments.

Classical ballet always has been, and still is, an art of rules. It is an academic art. If you observe the rules, they give you strength and confidence to attack any challenge. Rules are the foundation upon which to build a reliable technique. This is common with all activities that demand a high level of skill. However, many so-called contemporary theorists would try to convince us that times have changed and that these rules are old-fashioned and should be discarded to allow for innovations. They claim that the old concepts of classical ballet are outdated and that we should make room for new ideas. But remember Martha Graham's insistence that either the foot is pointed or it is not. Her admonition applies equally to straightening the knees, turning out the legs, maintaining a correctly placed basic stance, and dancing precisely with the music.

It is reported that Igor Stravinsky once said that he had a profound admiration for classical ballet, "which in its very essence, by the beauty of its order and aristocratic austerity of its forms, so closely corresponds with my conception of art. In classical dancing I see the triumph of studied conception over vagueness, of the rule over the arbitrary, of order over the haphazard."

Stravinsky's insight about ballet shares with all the arts a sense of the value of rules. In music, there is order in an orchestrated symphony. In painting, the artist re-creates the beauties of life and nature in ways that either overtly or subtly demonstrate a sense of order. And the poet provides cadence and rhythm to a unique turn of words. In dance, it is this insistence of the rule over the arbitrary that enables the dance artist to present his or her art in a clean, orderly manner, free of vagueness and the clutter of untutored and uncontrolled movement.

As with all ideas and theories, art is perceived uniquely by different interpreters, as well as by supporters and critics. It is analogous to looking at a stained-glass window. While one person gets a certain impression while viewing the window from the outside, another person may view the same window from the inside, getting a uniquely different perception of the beauty of the work. It is essential to be open to the possibility of changing one's perception, so as to gain greater insights.

Rules aid students in guiding them to master new challenges. In virtually every instance, dancers who have successfully transcended the artistic and technical difficulties inherent in their art have discovered that classical ballet is revealed by applying rules through work—days and days of work that become years of discipline work—never drudgery, but instead a joyful endeavor in the pursuit of ever-elusive perfection.

Wise artists in any field realize that perfection is not attainable. But to aspire to the highest levels of artistic achievement, one must continually work toward that impossible goal, while keeping in mind that there is always room for improvement, regardless of what audiences or critics say. Working at perfecting one's abilities through the application of established rules and newfound discoveries is not tilting at windmills. It is precisely that stimulation which ignites the passion to reach ever higher.

If one becomes complacent with plateaus already attained, then he or she is doomed to mediocrity. And there is nothing more deplorable in the arts than mediocrity. The pursuit of perfection is always the key to resolving this conundrum. But how can conscientious dancers and choreographers discover the pathway that leads to excellence? It all begins with teachers and the importance of their work.

Ballet teachers inherit the onus bequeathed to them by their mentors and past masters. Truly dedicated teachers who meet this responsibility will discover new heights of discovery that offer tempting hints of perfection, far in the distance perhaps, out of reach, but nevertheless evident. What a rewarding challenge!

CHAPTER 5   *Recommended Lesson Format for*
             Intermediate Levels and Above

I don't know why you are so excited.
After all, she is just an ordinary goddess.

Alexander Tolstoy, commenting on Galina Ulanova's
debut at the Kirov Theater in Leningrad

The following is a suggested format for organizing a lesson. It is a typical plan
that would be appropriate for intermediate levels and above.

First of all, it is always wise for students to warm up before the lesson begins. However, they must be taught the differences between warming up and
stretching, which are altogether different functions having different goals.
The guiding rule should be to warm up before the lesson and stretch afterwards. Warm-up exercises are those that move the body in simple, stress-free,
repetitive ways designed to provide heat to feet, ankles, knees, hips, hands,
wrists, elbows, shoulders, neck, back, and torso. There should never be stress
applied to these areas when the body is cold. Repetitive movement of flex-
ation and straightening in these areas provides heat that makes the demanding balletic movements of the lesson more easily executed. And, most important, a good warm-up helps to avoid injury.

Next, since the ballet lesson is the students' theatrical "event," it is necessary for them to get into an appropriate artistic frame of mind. Teachers
should never assume that the students are completely focused on the work
at hand. They often need to be shaken (although gently) out of their mundane stupors. This can be done very easily by beginning each lesson with a
révérence (theatrical bow)—one to their teacher and one to their accom-

panist (or to their imaginary audience in the absence of an accompanist). Also, when the teacher enters the classroom, it would be appropriate for the murmur of student conversations to end and for them to stand quietly and attentively while they await the teacher's signal to begin the lesson.

Assuming that their students either do not warm up properly or fail to do so at all, some teachers begin their lesson following the révérence with a set pre-barre warm-up exercise. This is done while facing the barre holding with both hands and employs many of the desired repetitive warm-up movements alluded to above. If this option is chosen, the teacher must think through what movements will accomplish the warm-up quickly and efficiently. It would be appropriate to repeat this same exercise before each lesson exactly the same way. That way no time is lost in explaining new exercises from day to day.

Learning classical ballet through repetitive exercises over a period of years is the tried and proven formula for attaining professional skills. It assumes that students are taking daily lessons. Therefore, it is not always necessary to do every exercise to completion because the total number of repetitions will balance out over time. This assumes, of course, that the teacher is cognizant of the need for such balance.

With this in mind, some teachers do their first barre exercise (grand plié) only on one side, with the other side being done on alternate days. Thus the grand plié exercise is done on the right side (holding the barre with the left hand) on Monday, Wednesday, and Friday, and on the left side (holding the barre with the right hand) on Tuesday, Thursday, and Saturday. In the "good old days" of ballet instruction, teachers would often have students do three or four grand pliés in each position on both sides. This represents up to thirty-two pliés every day, which is a far too heavy dosage to begin each barre with.

RECOMMENDED BARRE

Regardless of the option chosen by the teacher for grand pliés, the following suggested first exercise can easily be done exactly the same way in every lesson. I begin my lessons as follows:

1. In first position—demi-plié in four counts (outside arm remains in second position, inside hand holds the barre); cambré back in four counts (outside

arm moves through first position, third position, and back to second position, the head is turned away from the barre); grand plié in four counts; relevé in one count; return down in one count; tendu to second position in two counts.

2. In second position—demi-plié in four counts; cambré toward the barre in four counts (while holding the barre with the inside hand, raise the outside arm from second position to third position and return to second position, turn the head toward the barre); grand plié in four counts; relevé in one count; return down in one count; tendu and rond de jambe to fourth position in two counts.

3. In fourth position—demi-plié in four counts; let go of the barre and execute a stylized fourth port de bras beginning with both arms in first position (inside arm forward, outside arm backward arabesque style, head is slightly turned and inclined toward the barre); after returning to the original position with one hand on the barre, grand plié in four counts; relevé in one count; return down in one count; tendu and close fifth position in two counts. (Note: Check my first book or other Vaganova syllabus source to see description of a fourth port de bras.)

4. In fifth position—two demi-pliés in two counts each, combined with a single half port de bras; grand plié in four counts; and third port de bras in eight counts keeping the inside hand on the barre. (The exercise may end here. Other options are to quickly turn on both legs toward the barre and repeat the exercise on the other side without stopping the music; or relevé and hold a balance in fifth position with both arms in third position.)

This first exercise is an excellent way to begin the barre. It contains many useful ingredients and prepares the students for the exercises to follow. Since it repeats every day as the first combination, no explanation is required, and this speeds up the time required for the barre. Remember, our goal is to finish the entire barre in approximately thirty minutes for intermediate and advanced students.

Other ways to accomplish this is to do both sides of many exercises without stopping the music. This is accomplished through the use of half turns that are built into the choreography. In addition to simple turns on both legs, other ways to do half turns at the barre are tombés en tournant, coupés en tournant, fondus en tournant, half pirouettes, fouettés, flic-flacs, changements en tournant, etc. The choreography for such exercises must include ample music time to prepare, followed by the execution, and then preparation for beginning the exercise on the other side.

The following is a recommended order of basic exercises for the barre after completing the first grand plié exercise:

1. Battements tendus with and without plié.
2. Battement tendu jeté.
3. Rond de jambe à terre.
4. Battement fondu and/or battement soutenu.
5. Frappé and double frappé.
6. Rond de jambe en l'air.
7. Petit battement sur le cou-de-pied and battement battu.
8. Adagio with battement développé, relevé lent, demi and grand rond de jambe développé, large poses, etc.
9. Grand battement jeté.

In addition to the above basic formats, there are many complications, including turns that can be added to most of the above. Mentioned above are only the basic ingredients that the exercises are based upon. While we should not add complexities for the purpose of confusing students, they provide coloration and enrichment to routine exercises that are done more or less the same way every day, while challenging the students to reach for higher levels of dominion of their technique. In addition, many exercises are done on demi-pointe that are designed to strengthen the legs and feet and lead the students to more advanced levels of balance control. However, it is not advisable to turn the daily barre exercise into a series of choreographic puzzles. Keep in mind that the barre's main purpose is to prepare students for the work in the center.

The barre should challenge the mental acuity of students. It should never be so routine that it becomes boring. The old-school way of constructing most barre exercises was to make everything very square—"en croix" in ballet jargon—that is to say, an equal dose of movements executed front-side-back-side. The number of repetitions was nearly always done in multiples of four (four, eight, sixteen, thirty-two, etc.). Also, the waltz being commonly associated with dancing, 3/4 time was often used, even for exercises that needed more emphatic musical phrasing.

Vaganova saw through these weaknesses and made radical changes that proved her theories correct. Today, as in her time, products of her revolutionary methodology are both stronger and more flexible than their predecessors. In the past, the typical barre was rarely less than forty-five minutes, often lasting up to one hour. This left only forty-five to thirty minutes for essential center exercises, including the entire allegro portion of the lesson. Vaganova emphasized the importance of allegro as being the essence of dance. Therefore, only having time left to do two or three jumping combinations is grossly insufficient. It tends to make allegro appear to be not much more than an afterthought after a heavy dose of concentrated à terre exercises.

The only way to provide the necessary twenty minutes of time allotted for allegro in a typical ninety-minute lesson is to shorten the barre to thirty minutes and make sure that the center combinations do not run overtime. One might be tempted to say that you could also cut short the center portion of the lesson after an overly long barre. However, this would severely inhibit the use of exercises in the center that are designed to develop stability, balance, and strength as well as the vast repertoire of turns, épaulement, and other elements of "danciness" that are so essential to training a complete dance artist.

Imposing the "en croix mentality" on students is counterproductive. When doing a series of movements front-side-back-side, students are doing the movement twice as many times to the side as to the front and back (i.e. four times front, four times side, four times back, and again four times side). Not that this is a bad thing in itself, but over many years of training it is an unnecessary overload of repetitions to the side. It is also a simplistic way to accommodate the design of combinations that should include a variety of other important ingredients.

By doing the repetitions of movements with equal (or nearly equal) doses in the basic three directions, a final music phrase remains in which can be done other things, such as practice on small and large poses, balances, turns, port de bras, etc., all of which are important. By taking this approach the teacher will not need to design separate exercises to work on those other essentials, thus saving time.

Another very important identifying feature of a typical Vaganova-style lesson is the frequent use of odd numbers of repetitions—threes, fives, sevens, etc. This useful organizational tool not only helps to give important emphasis to conclusions of completed phrases as well as the beginnings of new phrases. This approach helps the student to wrap up, as it were, one part of an exercise, and then prepare to attack what follows with renewed focus.

There is nothing wrong with incorporating the preparation for an exercise in the music phrase itself, although it is common for preparations to take place before the exercise begins. Therefore, one could devise a combination that uses the first four counts of the musical phrase to prepare the arms, or to rise up onto demi-pointe, or to change from en-face to a pose incorporating épaulement.

It is now commonplace for many Russian teachers to conclude barre exercises in fifth position back. They begin the exercise in the normal way with the left hand on the barre, right foot in front in fifth position. But when the exercise ends the students finish with the right foot in back in fifth position rather than returning back to where they started from. This concept is viewed as a sign of completion.

It is also common for many Russian teachers to have their students finish each barre exercise by releasing their hold on the barre as they stand in fifth position with their arms held in the preparatory position (arms low). Depending on the exercise's choreography, this way of concluding sometimes requires the accompanist to interpolate a short music phase to accommodate the final movement's ending pose.

Even at the barre, exercises must always go through their designated movements to completion. This includes not only what the legs and arms are doing but also how the mind turns prosaic movements into artistic moments.

Students must be reminded that they must never allow themselves to drift into rote mindless routines, especially when overwhelmed by challenges. Remind them that such moments are to be expected and have to be dealt with and are an inevitable part of the process. Even after eight years of diligent study, each tendu and demi-plié must be executed with a mind and body that are alive and singing at all times. For students who have done 25,000 or 30,000 perfect pliés, each time they do another it must be done artistically as if for the first time. This is an especially difficult concept for teachers to instill in their students.

In the learning process, it is clear that mistakes will be made. The mind must be trained to move on from the possibility of errors and to focus on the demands of what follows. Built-in "holds" or "pauses" on the final count(s) of a music phrase facilitates this important aspect of learning. I am referring here to an ending pause on count 3 during a 4-count phrase; or count 7 of an 8-count phrase; or even on counts 6, 7, and 8 of an 8-count phrase.

In addition, it is not necessary to always do the same number of repetitions in each of the three primary directions. It is all right to do five repetitions each, front and back, and do seven to the side. Nothing terrible will happen with this seeming imbalance. Remember, the overall course of ballet instruction will last approximately eight years, and things will balance out in the long run—with proper planning.

Built-in pauses also afford students an opportunity to do necessary repair work to faulty balances, turnout, épaulement, the basic stance, etc. They also give students time to regroup and reorganize themselves to confront subsequent challenges in mid-exercise, and also to bring the exercises to a proper conclusion with an air of confidence and authority. These are important stagecraft concepts that must be learned along with improving technique and performance skills.

Combined, these elements help to create the potential for a complete artist. It would be too late to begin this process after graduation from school. One of the main causes for the proliferation of trainee and apprentice programs in the United States is that most graduating students simply do not have the professional look that company directors are looking for. Dancers ready for the stage evidence an air of authoritative self-confidence, in addition to artistic and technical skills. The simple device of adding pauses to exercises helps students confront these elements of professionalism.

RECOMMENDED CENTER

After the barre and before moving into the center, it is a good time to review certain important elements, such as the various pas de bourrées, additional port de bras and stretching exercises (especially ones where the leg is placed on the barre), relevés, and battement tendu pour batterie combinations. These should not be done every day, but occasionally, depending on what is being emphasized in the lesson plan.

The center exercise should consist of the following ingredients (or their equivalents):

1. Demi-plié, battement tendu, battement fondu/soutenu, développé/relevé lent, and grand battement should be done every day. It is assumed that épaulement is incorporated in each of the above. (See the Vaganova School dancing space diagram, available from several sources, including my earlier book.) All other barre exercises should be regularly rotated into the mix. All large and small poses must be incorporated on a regular basis in most exercises.

2. Once pirouettes and other turns are introduced, they should be inserted as an ingredient in most, if not all, of the above exercises.

3. Demi-pointe should be used extensively.

4. Once assimilated, many basic exercises are done en tournant.

5. The center should *always* include at least one fairly complex adagio combination consisting of a variety of ingredients. (A simpler shorter one can begin the center.) The grand adagio usually consists of a minimum of 64 measures of music, often 128 measures (even longer in advanced classes). Both sides and the reverse should be done. It should be the last or next to last exercise before the allegro begins. It is useful to repeat the grand adagio on successive days, as there are multiple ingredients that may not all be assimilated upon executing the combination on the first day.

RECOMMENDED ALLEGRO

During the years of elementary study students nearly always return to the barre to learn new allegro steps. This should be standard procedure. Once elements of new jumps are assimilated at the barre, they are brought out into the center to continue the work. Naturally, larger allegro steps and those that travel must be learned in the center, as holding the barre would inhibit movement. This is appropriate because basic allegro fundamentals have already been polished prior to introducing more complex jumps.

The recommended order of jumps is:

1. Small jumps on both feet: temps levé, changement, and échappé.

2. Small jumps from two feet onto one, one foot onto two, or from one foot to the other foot: assemblé, jeté, ballonné, and simple sissonne.

3. Small jumps with beats: échappé battu, single-beat entrechat (trois, royale, quatre, cinq), assemblé battu, and jeté battu.

4. Middle jumps: sissonne fermé, sissonne ouverte, and larger traveling assemblés and jetés.
5. Big jumps: grand jeté, grand fouetté sauté, grand assemblé, cabriole, grand sissonne ouverte, and tours en l'air.
6. Longer combinations of big and small jumps with and without beats, as well as other ingredients that comprise mini variations.
7. A final small allegro of repetitive fast jumps.

RECOMMENDED POINTE

It is much better for girls to receive pointe instruction in twenty- or thirty-minute segments several times a week rather than a one-hour pointe class once or twice a week. A one-hour dose of pointe work for girls who are unaccustomed to the discomfort is a heavy load. Their feet tend to hurt more. They form blisters more readily. And you run the risk of making some girls dread pointe work.

The Vaganova eight-year curriculum outline specifies precisely when and how to introduce pointe to the girls. The guideline is that pointe should be introduced only after the girls have begun to demonstrate that their feet, ankles, and legs are strong enough to support this work.

In the Russian schools, pointe is introduced to the girls in the first grade toward the end of the year. They are all close to or already eleven years old. Readers should also remember that they have been carefully selected for physical attributes and that their class meets six days a week. Under instruction with the same teacher, they have begun to demonstrate the requisite strength. Since all students are carefully selected, they potentially have the right feet and legs for this work. And many of their regular exercises are specifically designed to prepare them for pointe. They are already showing strength on demi-pointe, because they have been doing exercises to accomplish this goal for several months.

Before you decide that the great day has arrived, locate a shoe supplier who understands the intricacies of proper fitting. Pointe shoes are expensive. However, they are not shoes that one buys a little large to allow room to grow into. They must fit precisely.

Then, when everyone has their shoes, have the students bring them to class for you to check. Show them how to sew on the ribbons and also decide what type of toe pad they will use. It is also important to impress on them the importance of keeping their toenails cut short. A lapse here will lead to extreme discomfort and undesirable repercussions. After the ribbons are sewn, instruct them on how to tie the ribbons. (I strongly recommend that readers check my earlier book, which clearly illustrates an excellent method for tying ribbons.)

In the beginning, all pointe exercises should be taught facing the barre holding with both hands. The hands should be placed on the barre with all of the fingers on top and the hands touching each other. Make sure that the wrists and elbows relax. Resist the temptation to push down on the barre to help the relevé. In the beginning, work only on steps that rise onto both feet. Also in the beginning, do not attempt to sustain balances. A typical elementary pointe exercise might be (in first position): demi-plié on count 1; relevé on count 2; plié on count 3; and straighten up on count 4. Repeat no more than eight times. Then repeat or change to another position.

It is a teacher judgment call to decide when it is appropriate to bring exercises out into the center after they have been learned at the barre. The guideline should always be that such a move be made only after the students are able to exercise the movement(s) securely and safely while holding the barre and have demonstrated a certain level of dominion over the challenges. No compromises here.

In the "real world" of ballet instruction at levels any less than what has been described above, teachers must think first of the safety of their students before inviting them or encouraging them to begin working on pointe. In some cases, it may be completely inappropriate to have certain students even attempting to dance on pointe. This would especially be true of girls with feet and leg problems. This is an unfortunate reality that must be dealt with on an individual basis.

In cases where boys are taking classes together with girls, it is appropriate for the teacher to give them an extra jumping exercise or two while the girls are changing their shoes. This would be an appropriate time for the boys to work on exclusively male steps such as tours en l'air, additional pirouettes, and big jumps at slower tempos.

When a normal ninety-minute lesson contains pointe, it is essential that teachers find ways to save time, for example, by shortening the barre or by repeating allegro combinations from the previous lesson. Shortening the barre can be accomplished by making sure that the combinations are fairly simple and do not require extra time for demonstrations or explanations, especially in the case of new steps. Another time shortener for the barre is to do the same exercise on both sides without stopping the music. This is done by means of half-turns to change sides.

Another option is to cut the allegro segment short. In any case, it is essential that the girls do no fewer than three allegro combinations before changing for pointe. And they must learn how to change their shoes quickly. This is not the time for chitchat. My girls change their shoes in less than three minutes, with one especially proud girl ready to go in ninety seconds.

The final option for teachers who wish to include pointe in their daily lessons is to extend to two hours instead of the normal ninety minutes. This has the advantage that the girls will receive a full dose of allegro elements before changing their shoes. Also, the boys can review more elaborate combinations.

Due to the many distractions and demands placed on young students today, it is common for elementary students to only attend their class once or twice a week. This always results in extending the learning process by having to spend too much time on basic fundamentals. Then, in order to not lose the students to boredom, many teachers feel obliged to advance them at an inappropriate pace. This includes having students prematurely begin such elements as pirouettes and big jumps before they are ready to cope with the physical challenges.

Another downside to infrequent attendance is to put female students on pointe either too soon or too late. In either case, the necessary strength is not developed that is expected by company directors for professional work. Rather than rectifying this problem early on, directors have adopted the therapeutic remedy of having their dancers take daily company classes wearing pointe shoes. This tires the feet and ankles and can lead to injury. Instead, the problem should be attacked where the blame lies—during the early training years with daily lessons and correct teaching methodology.

Finally, it is a good idea to wind down each lesson with a simple port de bras exercise. And there is nothing wrong with ending it the same way every day, followed by a révérence the same as or similar to the one preceding the beginning of the lesson. Afterwards, I recommend that the students line up and shake the teacher's hand (together with a grateful "thank you") before exiting the studio. This allows the teacher an opportunity to offer congratulations or specific individual corrections. It also gives students an opportunity to ask questions.

It is occasionally beneficial for teachers to remain in the classroom with struggling students after the lesson ends. Sometimes students need a little extra help to grasp illusive ingredients. It gives teachers a one-on-one chance to focus exclusively on the efforts of a particular student without distractions. The student will appreciate your attention and feel special. However, be sure not to repeat this often with the same student, as others will undoubtedly be aware of what is happening and become curious. Avoid even the appearance of favoritism. Although possibly unwarranted, such special attention could lead to possible misunderstandings. It is best if every student feels that you care about them and want to help them achieve their goals.

CHAPTER 6   *Learning Process*

The purpose of art is to make the tensions
of life stand still, to be looked at.

Suzanne Langer

Many academies around the world are established to train dancers for professional companies. Some academies are training facilities for national companies that are subsidized by the host country. They may be fifty or a hundred years old, or they may have a much longer tradition, such as the Paris Opera School. Through many years of trial and error, most of these academies have come to the conclusion that it takes approximately eight years of daily training for talented ten-year-old beginners to be properly prepared for professional work. This approximate time frame has become the norm for national ballet companies in Russia, England, Cuba, Argentina, France, Denmark, and Canada, among others.

In addition, most of these countries have curriculums for training their teaching staffs in the methodologies they utilize, including Vaganova, Royal Academy, Cuban School, Paris Opera, and Bournonville. With rare exceptions, it is unthinkable for such academies to employ teachers who have no background other than as dancers, regardless of their longevity or fame. Aspiring teachers receive specific teacher training unique to the academy where they will work. This means, for example, that a Bournonville-trained teacher will not be on the staff of a Russian school. Every faculty member will have taken a course in pedagogy unique to the school that engages them. This prevents confusion and conflicts that could inhibit the smooth development of the students.

All of these schools audition thousands of students. Only the most likely candidates with professional proclivities are selected. Some of these academies even take a close look at potential students' parents to study the likely results of genes at work. It will be these students who in due course graduate into their associated companies and take the place of older dancers who gave their lives to the theater. Occasionally, a hugely talented graduate will take the place of a retiring great artist who has left their mark in ballet history. A past example of this is when Galina Ulanova retired from the Bolshoi Ballet Company. She took under her wing a young graduate from the school, Ekaterina Maximova, whom she then coached and nurtured until Maximova became a star in her own right.

It can be said that it is extremely difficult to get into one of these national academies, and students can be removed for a variety of reasons, not just for lack of talent. Only a small percentage of selected beginning students last through the program of study until they graduate. And even graduation does not guarantee entry into the company that the school is associated with. Such a level of selectivity maintains a high standard and provides outstanding artists for their countries' theaters. Sadly, this is not the case in the United States, where hundreds of schools employ thousands of teachers who provide training across a broad spectrum of quality, from excellent to dreadful.

In the United States, students who wish to learn the art of classical ballet face a confusing dilemma. How do they (or their parents) choose a teacher or a school when there are so many, with all claiming to be "the best"? The selection is made all the more difficult when the United States has no established standards to conform to, even in the most prestigious schools.

Virtually anyone can remodel the basement of their house, rent a storefront, or build a new ballet studio in a strip mall. Then, after hanging out a sign and placing ads in local newspapers, they only need to wait and see who shows up. There will always be some who inquire, usually beginning with those who live nearby. The success of many such endeavors largely depends on the budget given to advertising and promotion and the personality of the teacher, not necessarily professional qualifications.

Even the most conscientious parents are fooled by apparently valid credentials. But how does one check out a cleverly tweaked résumé? And does dancing with the local civic ballet company or even professional company experience qualify one to legitimately be called a teacher?

What about a degree in dance pedagogy from an accredited university dance program? This may be a better scenario, but most degree programs are not designed to prepare graduates for careers in dance at the professional level. This includes dance majors with a teaching emphasis. Institutions that emphasize modern dance or jazz do not qualify their graduates to teach classical ballet, and vice versa. One must always apply due diligence in investigating the track record of university dance departments. Always ask about how many graduates have been placed in companies or other professional work situations. Try to check up on the claim.

The following is an incident that took place in my school. One day we received an inquiry from a recent graduate of a well-known university dance department who had earned her degree with an emphasis on pedagogy. She explained that it was her fervent desire to find a teaching position where she could use her knowledge to help students achieve their dreams of dancing professionally. Could she visit our school and observe classes and possibly talk with us about her ambitions?

We invited her to visit anytime at her convenience. An appointment was arranged, and a few days later she arrived. She asked if she would be allowed to observe classes and take notes. My advanced preprofessional class was the last of the three she observed that day. Halfway through the barre she stopped taking notes and became less and less focused on her observations. By the end of the lesson she was holding her head in her hands. Afterward, as we began to talk, she broke down sobbing. After containing herself, she apologized and explained that, after watching our classes, she realized that she knew absolutely nothing about teaching classical ballet at anywhere near a professional level and that she had wasted four years and thousands of dollars at her alma mater. What a disgrace! The poor girl felt betrayed by false promises. Unfortunately, this is not an isolated example of what is happening in the United States.

However, rather than attempting to resolve this rather large conundrum in these pages, I will stick to offering suggestions to already established and novice ballet teachers who are focused on becoming more informed and better at their craft. It is to you that this book is dedicated.

Once an aspiring teacher has made the decision to learn the intricacies of the art, I would urge him or her to search out a pedagogue with a proper pedigree, one who has been trained how to teach and has a proven track record of preparing students for careers in professional companies. Even better, find a teacher who has demonstrated the ability to train up marginally talented students into professional company material. This is the sign of a real teacher. And remember, it does not cost any more to pay for the services of a highly skilled teacher than for a charlatan.

I hasten to add that not all students wish to become professional ballet dancers, just as not all retired ballet dancers should become teachers. There can be many reasons for putting oneself through the rigors of studying classical dance. And even those who have no desire to enter dance as a career deserve the very best learning experience that a well-prepared teacher is capable of giving. This applies even to adult students of advanced years. Teachers of adult students can find great satisfaction in working with mature students who always try their best and have an enviable work ethic.

It is worthwhile reiterating that it does not take great teaching ability to give maintenance classes to gifted students or professional dancers. "Class-givers" abound. Most are retired professional dancers who do not wish to stray far from the stage. They often congregate in large urban dance centers, where they compete with each other for popularity. Ironically, some of these "class-givers" could be outstanding teachers if they would only recognize that they have not yet learned the intricacies of how to teach, which is an art altogether different from performing.

Watching other teachers at work, attending seminars and conferences, earning an advanced degree, and having a serious desire are not in themselves enough to qualify one to teach. It is imperative to study the intricacies of pedagogy with a proven expert.

Yet another comment on "master teachers." They are a special breed who are able to attract "name" dancers to their classes due to their fame. There are some commonalities in their classes. They are usually entertaining, and they also help to maintain basic conditioning for those still active on the stage. However, it is rare that such classes offer meaningful challenges for students engaged in the learning process. Many longtime professional dancers no longer wish to feel the angst of struggling with complex exercises. They prefer to slide easily through the class. Corrections from such teachers occasionally help a dancer or student who is struggling with a technical problem or who lacks artistic quality in their movements. Some of these teachers might even have a keen eye for important details, and their words are worth listening to. However, that is not sufficient in itself.

Young, impressionable students who take classes from such teachers are often enchanted when they find themselves dancing alongside professional dancers. And to hear those wonderful pearls of wisdom pouring forth from the master's mouth is such a great privilege! However, as is often the case, not much genuine instruction takes place in these rather loosely organized classes. Often dancers arrive late and leave early; pick and choose which exercises to perform; dress however they please, covered head to toe with warmers; and drink coffee and gossip between exercises. For them, it is ballet social hour. Careful scrutiny is required.

It is rare that such masters are able to base their reputations on being known for training elementary students to the heights of stardom. They usually avoid beginner-level classes, which are too slow and uninteresting for them. Since they often attract professional dancers and preprofessional students through open classes, it is common for these teachers to be asked to mentor especially talented younger students. Parents are inevitably impressed by a master's offer to take their darling under his or her wing. The fact is that talent inevitably rises on its own, unless it is inhibited or damaged along the way. Probing this question will uncover many examples of outstanding dancers finding their own path in spite of rather mediocre teaching. Naturally, there are far greater benefits when a gifted student finds him or herself in the hands of a true pedagogue. Valuable time is preserved by not having to unlearn questionable or useless theories.

While not covering every aspect of quality teaching, the above generalities have steered us directly to the following discussions of some extremely important concepts that I hope will lead conscientious teachers to better results with their students. While perusing these pages, I ask that readers set aside previously accepted notions of instruction for the time being. Do not be tempted to compare methods or try to reconcile these concepts with already accepted theories of your own, unless they are consistent with what you already believe. This will facilitate incorporating the new ideas into dependable teaching techniques and hopefully awaken dormant understanding.

Keep an open mind. Don't be put off if I step on your toes or if criticism strikes home. Put these new ideas to the test in your classroom with your students before judging harshly. I can assure you that everything that follows has been proven to work.

CHAPTER 7

The Basic Stance

> Dance is communication. And so the great
> challenge is to speak clearly, beautifully,
> and with inevitability.
>
> *Martha Graham*

One cannot overemphasize the importance of The Basic Stance (TBS). Mastery of it is essential for achieving the highest levels of technical proficiency in classical ballet. For this reason all ballet teaching methodologies emphasize it, some more than others. The great twentieth-century Russian teacher Agrippina Vaganova considered the basic stance indispensable, and gave instructions to teachers to emphasize its importance, until there was no doubt that their students had mastered it.

Vaganova took her cue from the great ballet masters of the past who were onto something important when they discovered that the intricacies of classical ballet technique cannot be learned without understanding the principles of the basic stance. TBS is the foundation for everything a dancer does from the simplest demi-plié and battement to the most complex grand allegro leap.

Theories abound of what the proper basic stance should consist of. They are commonly stated with cursory explanations from less learned teachers. And they are occasionally explained utilizing unnecessarily complicated theories. However, I will present here a nearly foolproof method of learning this essential principle that all teachers and students should find useful.

First of all, it must be agreed that the basic stance is the foundation for every aspect of classical dance. Not only is TBS necessary for dancers to be able to execute each individual step properly, but also in combinations of the easiest to the most complex steps—in other words, whatever a ballet master or choreographer might envision. Dancers who master TBS feel that they are in complete control of their movements at all times, so that they only need to concentrate on the portrayal of the role or choreographic image they are performing. And, most important, they must appear to the viewer to be dancing with ease. Otherwise, the audience will not be able to enjoy their viewing experience. There is nothing worse—except for really bad dancing—than for the audience to be worried about whether or not a struggling dancer will be able to make it through their steps without faux pas. The audience pays well to see polished performances by professional artists, and they deserve nothing but the best.

Mastery of TBS comes from work in the classroom and a constant referral back to its important role by knowledgeable teachers. Even company directors and ballet masters who take an active role in rehearsing their companies must be thoroughly conversant with its essentials. It should never be assumed that many years as a student combined with years of dancing in a professional company guarantees dominion of TBS or even an accurate interpretation of it.

In the Vaganova syllabus, TBS holds an extremely important place. Learning its requirements begins with ten-year-old elementary students on their very first day of lessons. It continues to be emphasized and reemphasized for as long as it takes for students to internalize and thoroughly understand its importance. Eventually, students learn that nothing will work properly if it is not founded on the requisites of the basic stance.

In my previous book, *Teaching Classical Ballet,* I gave a detailed description of the basic stance as follows:

THE BASIC STANCE

Great care should be taken to teach every beginner the basic stance (TBS). The specific details of TBS are learned in the beginning while facing the barre. They are as follows:

> BODY WEIGHT: Should be distributed evenly over the whole foot, with approximately 60 percent over the balls of the feet and 40 percent over the heels.

FEET: In the beginning, feet are placed in a relaxed (no turnout) first position (side by side with heels together).

ANKLES: Evenly align on both the outside and inside of the leg and firmly support the shin bones above the arches of the feet.

KNEES: Although the legs must be held straight, the knee joints must not be allowed to lock at their rearward extreme. This is particularly important for students with hyperextended joints. The knee should help form and control a straight legline extending from the ankle to the pelvis.

THIGHS: All four muscle groups (inner, front, outer, and rear) are pulled up under the pelvis, as if trying to lift the body upwards.

PELVIS: With the abdominal muscles active and the muscles of the buttocks held firmly, vertically align the pelvic block beneath the lower back. Do not allow the buttocks to be pushed or tucked under.

BUTTOCKS: Keep gluteus muscles firmly flexed.

SOLAR PLEXUS: Abdominal muscles simultaneously lift and "grip" the lower rib cage.

The above ingredients of TBS form the foundation of proper and safe turn-out. They are also essential to the use of one's full lung capacity, and they aid in eliminating the problem-causing arched lower back, which in turn results in loss of stability in balances and in the more complex turning and jumping movements.

Additional essential TBS ingredients are:

HANDS: Palms down, with fingers extended and lightly resting on top of the barre, wrists and elbows relaxed.

ARMS: A comfortable arm's length from the barre, reaching straight forward, shoulder-width apart.

TORSO: Shoulders and hips held horizontal—the right shoulder directly above the right hip and the left shoulder directly above the left hip.

RIB CAGE: Lower front portion held closed by the upper abdominal muscles.

CHEST: Lifted, projecting outward and upward to allow for efficient breathing.

SHOULDERS: Held down and pulled somewhat back, so the shoulder blades are flat across the back, but not pinched together.

NECK: Straight and aligned vertically above the spine and over the center of the torso when seen from the rear.

HEAD: Pulled up on the neck, eyes looking straight forward.

The student must consciously feel that the upper body is over the top of— dominating—the lower body. TBS, sometimes called "placement," is the foundation of ballet technique and is indispensable for attaining the highest levels of technical proficiency.

Another test may be given by teachers to check the student's alignment. This test utilizes the principle of a carpenter's tool called the "plumb bob" or "plumb line," which is used to determine precise verticality. It is a simple device consisting of a length of string that is weighted at one end while being held above the floor by the other end. When the weight ceases to swing and the string is motionless, the string hangs precisely vertically due to gravity.

When observed from the side, an imaginary plumb line extending downward to the floor from the top of the student's head should sequentially intersect with the student's ear, the center of the student's shoulder, followed by the hip, knee, and ankle joints. Also, the spine should parallel the same vertical plumb line but not lie directly on it. In addition, if the student is balancing on demi-pointe (on the balls of the feet) or on full pointe, the plumb line will also intersect with these areas of the foot as the imaginary line ultimately contacts the floor.

On demi-pointe, with the weight on the balls of the feet, each of the toes should press firmly into the floor. In this way, together with the ball of the foot, the toes create a sort of miniplatform to stand on, thus helping to stabilize balance. This use of the toes is essential for learning all varieties of balances, from the simplest to the most complex, especially for pirouettes. In addition, a high demi-pointe should be used, so that the arch of the instep is clearly visible.

Finally, although reiterated ad nauseam, the admonition to "pull up" is not merely a cliché. With respect to demi-pointe it is essential. Tell your students to "cheat the scale and become two pounds lighter."

Each aforementioned body part should be stacked up in layers, as it were, one above (or below) each adjacent part. Meanwhile, the muscles that surround and/or affect these skeletal building blocks must be engaged in an efficient manner to "connect" and hold the aligned body parts together—but without tension.

It can be stated that nothing will work properly if the basic stance is not recognized as the foundation for all classical ballet positions and movements, from the simplest to the most complex. Teachers of elementary students must take whatever time is necessary for their students to comprehend and accept TBS's importance. It is also important to mention here that most students younger than about eight or nine are unable to feel and control the aforementioned various body parts involved, and are consequently unable to assimilate the essentials to a point of usability in their work on dance steps, except for the most elementary ones. This is why the schools in Russia do not begin formal elementary training until the age of ten.

Note: Several schools of classical ballet instruction from the former Soviet republics (pre-1990), including the Russian Academy of Ballet in St. Petersburg and the Moscow Academy of Dance, now include a pre-ballet class before the formal eight-year syllabus program of study begins. This helps to identify talented children earlier and also gives them a head start in learning fundamentals. The result of this innovation is a somewhat accelerated syllabus that has been in place during the last few years, whereby each class moves at a slightly faster pace through the syllabus because of the "head start."

Although Russian pre-ballet classes are kept simple for the most part, the students are also taught some fundamentals of elementary training from the regular syllabus's first-year class. This gives teachers an opportunity to observe other intangibles such as students' ability to concentrate, their demeanor, their receptivity to the strict regimen, and their musicality.

Back to TBS. Since students are physically unable to see their own alignment from the side, it is incumbent on teachers to explain, re-explain, enforce, reinforce and re-reinforce (ad infinitum, even ad nauseam) the importance of this most imperative requirement, until such time that the students can feel and control what their bodies are doing. Students will never reach their maximum potential without perfecting the basic stance. Teachers must make sure that it assumes a primary place of importance in their list of goals to achieve for elementary students.

It goes without saying that TBS is more easily learned and controlled while performing stationary movements. However, complete control of all moving ballet steps, especially jumps and the multitude of turning movements, must incorporate this all-important technical requirement. Then, once TBS is established, involuntary reactions must not be allowed to contaminate efforts to execute intended movements. In fact, it should be emphatically stated that there should never be any involuntary movements.

All movements, whether static or traveling, on the floor or in the air, must always be precisely directed by the conscious or subconscious mind. Unintended reactions that would disrupt intentioned movements must be strictly eradicated. Such involuntary reactions inevitably require repair work to correct misalignment, balance problems, etc., and they only serve to make the intended movements more challenging than necessary, causing viewers to sense the effort rather than being able to relax and enjoy the result.

Well-trained dancers, under the watchful eye of knowledgeable teachers, are able to overcome the troublesome struggle with reactions without undermining intended actions. Dancing, no matter how challenging the technical demands, then becomes a joy to perform for the executant and an uplifting and unforgettable viewing experience for the audience, especially when combined with artistic and aesthetic ingredients. Dancing creates a theatrical communication and mutual bond between the giver and the receiver. Under competent tutelage, it is incumbent on all students and performers to strive to master the demands of this high goal.

CHAPTER 8   *Balance Imperatives*

Finding the art in dance chisels an indelible image
in the mind of the beholder and also the performer.

A. Sage

Balance is one of those tiresome words one hears over and over in nearly every ballet classroom around the world. Even mediocre teachers are aware of its importance. It is doubtful that there has ever lived a ballet teacher who has not used this term repeatedly. However, when a teacher admonishes students to hold their balance, unless he or she explains what this means in greater detail, the students may be mystified about how to accomplish this.

Balance is directly associated with the vertical plumb line concept previously discussed in chapter 7. Balance is a simple concept of physics, whereby an object's weight distribution is aligned in such a way as to allow the object to effortlessly stand on its vertical axis without any lateral pressures that may interrupt or affect vertical alignment.

With the human body, this is relatively simple as long as the principles of the basic stance are rigorously employed. However, things change when the body begins to move or when parts of the body leave their "neutral" positions or shift from position to position, whether voluntarily or involuntarily. These complications continually challenge dancers' ability to control their movements, which is why it takes so long to learn how to dance well.

Since movement (changing arm and leg positions, both statically in one place or while traveling along the floor or in the air) is inherent to dance, weight distribution and alignment must also change. Thus balance is in a constant state of flux as the dancer moves around the floor. Nevertheless, balance is a critical control issue and must be dealt with at all times. In the beginning, students must learn to control balance consciously. And sometime during the intermediate years of study (years four through six of an eight-year program) they should be able to do so without thinking.

One can readily understand this while observing infants as they learn how to stand, walk, and run. They gradually learn to transfer their weight toward the direction they want to go. At first, when too much weight is moved, they either fall or they hurry to "catch up" with their moving weight. With time and experience, they learn how to manipulate just the right amount of weight, and their efforts become streamlined and less effortful. Dance in general, and classical ballet in particular, complicates these concepts enormously.

In the beginning, while the fundamentals for elementary ballet students are simple, balance is not so demanding. Most things are done while standing on both feet. But as each stage of development leads to new challenges, teachers constantly test their students' ability to control what they are learning. Balance can then become especially troublesome.

It is incumbent on all teachers to press the concept of ever increasing challenges, so that students are never allowed to lazily drift through the comfort zone. When challenges disappear, students tend to become complacent. Remember that a dancer's value to a ballet company director or a choreographer is acknowledged when he or she is capable of doing anything that is asked, no matter how eccentric the pose or movement. And the movements must be done with control so they can be repeated at will.

As teachers raise the level of difficulty, the demands of controlling the basic stance and balance are dramatically increased. Nevertheless, students must be in control of their balance at all times, not just during or between challenging moments. For example, if they are in perfect balance during the plié preparation before a pirouette begins, they are more likely to be in balance during and after the pirouette, as long as no involuntary reaction is allowed to corrupt an efficient relevé onto demi-pointe (or pointe).

The same principle applies to every terre-à-terre movement and jump. It does not matter where the arms or the legs go. Changing the position(s) of these extremities may have a minor or even a major effect on overall balance. However, through repetition, students gradually learn how much deviation from the true verticality of the basic stance each movement requires. Some students learn this quickly. They seem to feel their alignment more easily, while others must diligently and persistently work at it.

The following is an example of a simple involuntary reaction that is often seen in struggling students. It is evidenced by a lifting and separation of the rib cage from the abdomen muscles that sometimes happens when the arms are quickly raised overhead.

Another example of an involuntary reaction occurs as a result of initiating a relevé from a preparatory plié. It manifests itself as a "heaving" of the chest upward to help lift the weight of the torso. The result of this erroneous movement is to shift the shoulders backward, behind the required vertical plumb line.

Ironically, students can learn to control their balance in spite of these aberrations by compensating shifts of weight forward with the hips or backward with the shoulders. However, such adjustments only compound the problem. If left uncorrected, such compound reactions serve to make dancing infinitely more complicated than it needs to be.

Even the most elementary exercises at the barre can be corrupted by involuntary reactions. For example, if the pelvis is allowed to tilt forward while executing a demi-plié, there will inevitably be three compensating reactions: (1) the knees will push forward, (2) the lower back will arch, and (3) the shoulders will react backward in an attempt to control the forward weight shift. Though undesirable, these movements will be necessary in order to maintain what may feel like a semblance of balance. However, the basic stance is lost, and the body will be unable to control any complex movement.

Remember this admonition: There should never be any involuntary reaction to any action. Everything must be done on purpose, never by accident.

Balance is also a prerequisite for the execution of jumps. In every jump there are three critical moments of balance: balance precisely at the moment of the takeoff from the floor, balance at the apex of the jump, and balance on the landing. While these might seem obvious, the three (as a whole) are often overlooked. This is because jumps that travel do not pause long enough upon taking off from the floor to check the critical moment of balance. Neither do they last long enough while traveling through the air to check balance at the apex, since they are usually combined with other challenges to deal with. And then, after landing, there are generally other steps that follow or poses to hold that command attention.

Regardless of the above demands, if balance is not controlled during all three critical moments of a jump, the leaper will look and feel out of control to some extent. While the casual observer might not be sophisticated enough to discern the problem, a knowledgeable viewer's keen eye will be able to detect it. If left unattended for too long, bad habits will form, and the dancer will no longer be able to feel problems associated with questionable balances. Bad habits will become "old friends" and begin to feel natural. This must be avoided at all costs.

CHAPTER 9

Jumping Imperatives

You must develop great strength to make great
leaps. No chasm can be crossed with small jumps.

Vernon d'Evans

While it is true that there are natural jumpers, all students can be taught how to jump in an efficient and balanced way. When this is accomplished, the student can then embark on a strength-building regimen to increase the power potential of jumping. Thus a correct approach to jumping, when combined with added strength, results in an effective and impressive leaping ability, fulfilling Agrippina Vaganova's demand on the importance of allegro in classical dance.

In the ballet world, one repeatedly hears the centuries-old instructions: turn out, pull up, and balance. As conscientious teachers discover, the great ballet masters of the past knew something about this mysterious art when they emphasized these three imperatives. These sometimes tiresome admonitions are, in fact, urgent requirements. If they are taken for granted or brushed aside, then the student/dancer is doomed to failure, either by suffering recurring injuries, stagnated progress, or—worse yet—bad dancing. Conscientious students must always pay strict attention to their teacher's urgings, thereby facilitating improvement and progress.

All well-trained teachers know that progress in learning classical ballet is based on the students' mastery of alignment. It can be said that nothing can work properly without a thorough understanding and mastery of this fundamental. The basic stance demands that students stand with all of their body parts aligned—ankles over feet, knees over ankles, hips over knees, shoulders over hips, and ears over shoulders. With this foundation the arms can be placed in almost any configuration without disturbing balance, and we can move in any direction without losing this core foundation, which is essential for jumping.

Jumps (allegro steps) are separated into three main types—strictly vertical, strictly horizontal, and a mixture of vertical and horizontal. They are also separated into three sizes—petite, middle, and grand (small, medium, and large). Each jump has its own concomitant balance issues. And it is incumbent on teachers not only to teach each step but also to show how balance is used to accomplish the step's goal efficiently. Finally, in spite of what some teachers say, there is really only one optimal way to accomplish each step, even though there seem to be a multitude of theories, all of which are somewhat less effective than the *one*.

Effective powerful jumping in classical ballet follows Isaac Newton's third law of motion, which states that "for every action there is an equal and opposite reaction." With regard to jumping, this means that the primary action that impels the jump (push against the floor) must result in an equal and opposite reaction (departure from the floor), whether vertical, lateral, or both. The only mitigating factor is that the speed of the push from the floor determines how high or how far the jump will travel.

It is therefore incumbent on teachers to instruct students in such a way as to increase the strength and speed of their jumping movements from the bottom of the preparatory plié to the apex or highest point of the jump. Naturally, the extent of the push is proportionate to the intended size and shape of the jump. A good exercise to strengthen this ability is as follows:

1. (Music: In one measure of moderate 4/4 time.) On the upbeat before count 1—while standing in first position facing the barre, with hands resting on the barre shoulder width apart—energetically dégagé the right leg to the side at a height of 45 degrees without shifting balance.

2. On count 1—with a push from the supporting leg—tombé sideways into a deep demi-plié slightly beyond the dégagé of the working foot. (Keep the supporting leg stretched with the toe on the floor. All of the body's weight shifts into the tombé with the knee directly over and in line with the foot.)

3. On count 2—using the thigh muscles—push off powerfully from the working leg as quickly as possible. Point the foot sharply as in step 1 above. Return back to balance over the supporting leg (whole foot on the floor).

4. On count 3—return the working leg to first position.
5. On count 4—hold.
6. Repeat seven times with the same leg, hold the eighth measure, and then change legs.

Important Reminders: Allow the hands to move along the barre so that they remain shoulder width apart at all times. Turn the head sideways and look in the direction of the tombé. Then look straight forward when returning to first position. Do not allow the torso to twist into the tombé. As this exercise is assimilated, it can be done adding increasing difficulties, that is, from fifth position on the whole foot, from fifth position on demi-pointe, and also adding beats with the working leg energetically crossing in front of and behind the supporting leg.

When done with beats, jumps must be done aggressively, with the legs making quick, sharp calf-muscle contact with each other in deeply crossed fifth positions (no need to place the working heel on the floor). When done in this form, the combined movement is called "battement tendu pour batterie," which is also a preparation for entrechats and pas battus. This can be complicated with one or more beats utilizing the rhythm pattern for single-beat steps (e.g., entrechat quatre) and also for double-beat steps (e.g., entrechat six).

The appropriate time during a lesson to do this exercise would be at the end of the barre before moving into the center. It may also be done prior to the first allegro exercise or at the end of the lesson after the final allegro exercise.

In addition to petits battements sur le cou-de-pied and battements battus, the fast beating aspects of the battement tendu pour batterie exercise help to train "quick twitch" muscular responses for other petite allegro demands. Naturally, the principles that these exercise employ must be later incorporated into jumping combinations in the center of the room.

The foregoing exercise sequence is very useful in developing the strength and quick reactions evidenced by a powerful jump. When done consistently it has been proven to turn lead-legged "nonjumpers" into soaring leapers.

As has been previously stated, all static poses and positions and moving steps incorporate a comprehensive understanding of how to use the basic stance, and we have shown that TBS is the foundation of balance control. The reason why learning how to become a dancer takes approximately eight years of persistent study is that the myriad of moving steps, and their seeming endless combinations, challenge the students' ability to maintain their control of TBS and balance as one movement connects with another. In fact, it is incumbent on teachers to make their students confront these often uncomfortable and seemingly impossible (at that particular moment in a student's development) challenges.

Even conscientious students may resent such impositions of discomfort. Nevertheless, this is the only way for students to discover how good they are at any given moment and how good they can become. Ultimate success stems from small victories. Good teachers find ways to help their charges overcome difficulties and stay on track. As students search for the "Eureka!" moment of each challenge, small successes will lead, little by little, to greater discoveries, until students finally become dancers. Meanwhile, the struggle continues.

Another aspect of Vaganova's method for learning classical ballet is that, in the beginning, virtually everything that students do is first learned facing the barre while holding the barre with both hands shoulder width apart. This includes nearly all basic jumping steps.

Most exercises are first learned to the side. Next, as they are assimilated, they are done to the rear. Then they are done to the front holding with one hand while facing along the barre. Finally, they are executed in the center. This systematic method of introducing new stages of development is utilized for nearly all steps. In most cases the change from one phase of difficulty to another is entirely dependent on the teacher's discretion. And teachers should *not* be in a hurry to move ahead, as premature advancement leads to a common problem. Students understand what they are supposed to do, but they are unable to execute challenging new movements correctly, which can lead to frustration and the creation of bad habits. It is advisable for teachers to progress slowly, keeping in mind that everything students attempt in the beginning may be confusing and difficult. Have patience.

Following the above procedure for learning new steps means that every new jump that is executed in place, even though it may be based on a jump previously learned, requires that students initially return to the barre, where they learn the new fundamentals while facing the barre holding with both hands.

Again how long students remain doing new jumps at the barre before taking them out into the center is a judgment call by the teacher. Don't be in a hurry! It may only be one or two lessons for simple steps like temps levés or changements. On the other hand, it may take several lessons before assemblés should be attempted in the center. Jumps that have a traveling requirement must by necessity be learned in the center. However, most of these come much later in the study sequence and also incorporate more complex use of the arms and legs.

Teachers must be thoroughly acquainted with the differences between petite, middle, and grand allegro jumps. There is rarely a crossover in dynamic emphasis between them. That is to say, for example, that sissonne fermé is a middle jump, *not* a grand allegro step. Therefore, it is incorrect to teach it as a maximum effort leap. However, certain other jumps can be both petite and grand in form, such as pas jeté, sissonne ouverte, or assemblé. Not only is there a dynamic power difference between the large and small versions of these steps, but participating arms are specifically held either in the small poses or the large poses accordingly. In other words, it would be incorrect for a small jump to be done with a big pose of the arms, or a big jump to be done with the arms in small poses. This is a reliable rule that all teachers should understand and pass on to their students. I hasten to add that there are exceptions to nearly every "rule." However, exceptions should never be incorporated into normal learning sequences.

It would take an entire book to analyze every jump and provide instruction on how to execute each one. This is not my intent here. Therefore, I recommend that all teachers obtain a copy of *School of Classical Dance* by Vera Kostrovitskaya and Alexei Pisarev. This is the definitive "how to" book that covers virtually every aspect of teaching classical ballet technique including elementary and advanced forms of many steps. Based on Agrippina Vaganova's methodology, it is the serious teacher's "Bible" and is required reading for all teachers.

Vera Kostrovitskaya was Vaganova's assistant teacher. Following Vaganova's death in 1951, Kostrovitskaya was the senior teacher at the Vaganova Academic Choreographic School in Leningrad. (Today the school, located on Rossi Street in St. Petersburg, is called the Russian Academy of Ballet and is directed by a famous former Kirov ballerina, Altinai Asylmuratova.) Kostrovitskaya was instrumental in helping to establish the methodology throughout the entire Soviet Union. Alexei Pisarev was a pupil of the renowned Vladimir Ponomaryov and, for many years, a teacher at the Vaganova School and also for the Kirov Ballet Company.

Continuing our study of jumping, it is indispensable to maintain all of the correct aspects of TBS during the jump, regardless of whether or not the step is meant to be executed in one place or traveling. Since it is easier to maintain TBS without the additional challenge of traveling (shifting weight), all jumps are always taught in isolation, that is, one at a time with separate preparations and endings. Also, tempos should be very slow in the beginning, using easily defined meter such as 4/4 or 2/4.

As students begin this process, they learn that a certain effort is required to create the correct preparatory plié that initiates all jumps. It is a moment of engaged readiness with the body and mind preparing to attack the movements that follow. Muscles are preparing to respond, and the mind is ready to direct the required actions of the step. In the beginning, to form accurate correct patterns of movement, many of these preparations must be consciously directed. Later, with assimilation, everything will coordinate subconsciously.

As the study of jumps proceeds, students must also be taught how to overcome the tendency to collapse, or deflate as it were, when descending into the landing plié of each jump. Teachers are aware that most new jumpers tend to lose the ability to maintain their basic stance as the jump returns to the floor. This is a common challenge. To overcome this tendency, students must be taught to continue pulling up even as they are descending into the plié. This is a rule that carries over into many other aspects of learning to dance. Teacher vigilance is required to help students overcome this natural tendency.

Learning the basics of jumping begins at the barre with other much simpler related movements such as battements tendus with demi-plié, where the legs close into a solid fifth position while simultaneously entering the concluding plié. It should be obvious that this series of simple actions on the floor relates directly to pas assemblés in the center.

Other common barre exercises that relate directly to jumping are battements fondus and battements soutenus, which employ a continuous repetition of alternating pliés and relevés on the same supporting leg. The direct correlation between battements fondus and pas ballonés should become clear as ingredients of the basic stance and a pulled-up body are maintained, even while descending into each plié. The same applies to the actions of battements soutenus that relate directly to sissonnes ouvertes. The only ingredients missing from these barre exercises are the speed of the attack and the spring off the floor which their jumping "cousins" utilize. Therefore, battements tendus, battements fondus, and battements soutenus should be seen as preparations for the jumps they are related to.

This leads us to one of Vaganova's most important discoveries. She recognized the direct relationship between seemingly ordinary exercises routinely done at the barre as warm-ups and their jumping equivalents. By emphasizing certain important aspects, including the use of demi-pointe in many barre exercises, she was able to guide her students to stronger and more stable jumping techniques. Stability in jumping depends on aplomb, strength, and a solid but supple demi-plié. A popular term used by many Russian teachers for this combination of strength and suppleness is "plastic."

While the aspects of demi-plié are for the most part related to the legs and feet, aplomb and strength involve the entire body. Aplomb is directly related to the basic stance. It preserves the vertical alignment to allow the jump to work as efficiently as possible. However, elements of strength as they relate to jumping utilize the entire body, not just the legs. Strength is developed by repeating the movement, so that the muscles required to execute the movement are fortified and become stronger.

While jumps utilize the legs and feet, muscles of the torso, especially the abdomen, stomach, and back, are essential to providing a solid foundation for stable jumping as well. When these muscle groups are well trained, they help prevent unwanted reactions to the actions that the legs and feet provide. Especially critical are the landing moments when all related muscle groups must stabilize the reentry into the concluding demi-plié.

A lazy back will undermine the landing. The same is true with the stomach. The torso must be lifted while being supported by the legs underneath. Alignment must be preserved during the entire process. These principles are more easily learned during the practice of simple vertical jumps from two feet. Adding the element of travel greatly complicates the process. Therefore, students should not attempt traveling jumps until static ones are thoroughly understood and controlled. Again, moving on to more layers of complications is always a judgment call by the teacher.

Once static jumping theories are thoroughly understood and assimilated, we can advance to the study of traveling jumping steps. Here is where we begin to test the students' understanding of TBS, weight placement, and balance.

Also important in the study of jumping is the proper use of the arms. They must never be allowed to just go along for the ride. They are active participants, sometimes even motivators. The arms must not react to the effort of the legs. They participate in the initial departure from the floor, helping to gain the required elevation (altitude) of the leap. There must be no reflexive or wasted energy. The arms must move energetically as they help to propel the jump. Then, when the jump has done the work of impelling the required elevation, the arms hold their pose as the jump proceeds through the apex and into the landing, thus attaining the illusion of sustained flight.

Another necessary aspect of jumping is ballon, the French term for bounciness. It is when the dancer uses a light, elastic quality as jumps rebound one after another. It is analogous to the repeated rhythmical bouncing of a ball. Ballon is closely associated with petit allegro and some middle allegro jumps that do not have a strong traveling ingredient.

The theory of controlling traveling jumps is relatively simple. Once again, it is based on TBS, which must be maintained at all times. Otherwise, the shifting weight that is being transported by the various preparatory movements (e.g. glissade, chassé, pas de bourrée, pas couru, step-coupé, etc.) will induce a temporary misalignment of body parts and a consequent loss of basic placement. It must be understood that, if any of the vital body parts depart from the plumb line, proper balance is impossible, since balance is dependent on vertical alignment. However, a false balance can be constructed even on a foundation of misaligned parts. Teachers must be vigilant to strictly eradicate any such errors.

If any key body part that is required for proper alignment is not properly placed, a semblance of balance can be achieved only by misaligning other parts to compensate. However, false balances become less and less controllable as challenges increase. You can readily test this by having subjects stand at the barre and observe while they lift their leg in any direction to various heights. Monitoring closely, you will readily see that the subject must slightly adjust their body backwards if the leg is extended forward. Similar adjustments must take place when the leg moves backward or sideways. The amount of adjustment is affected by how high the leg is raised—only a little if the raised leg is below 45 degrees, more if the leg is raised to 90 degrees. These are acceptable adjustments that are controlled responses to correct the feeling of being out of balance as weight shifts. The subject is attempting to maintain his or her balance while weight is moving away from the vertical plumb line.

If done properly, the proper weight distribution of 60 percent over the balls of the feet and 40 percent over the heels can be maintained. Therefore, what is happening is that the subject is shifting just enough weight to counterbalance the momentary misalignment. This is acceptable procedure. However, if taken to the extreme, imbalance is caused by gross misalignment or overcompensation.

In the case of misaligned shoulders or hips—in order to create a "feeling" of balance—the subject's placement is altered and falsely corrected by a corresponding misalignment of adjacent or other nearby body parts, including weight distribution on the foot. Sometimes a minor corrective adjustment can be done by just a simple repositioning of the arms. In other instances, the weight shift may be accomplished by other means such as leaning or throwing the body in a direction that feels correct but that undermines the intended movement and is ultimately aesthetically unappealing.

To overcome any of these undesirable tendencies, teachers must pay close attention to their students' basic stance at all times. We must never assume that they have it, just because they can stand up straight or even balance on one or both feet. Remember, dancing onstage is not only posing beautifully but also moving through both simple and complex choreographed phrases effortlessly. Even so-called off balance movements onstage must give viewers a feeling that the dancer is in complete control. In this sense, control = balance and balance = control.

Meanwhile, each step has its concomitant requirements for maximum visual effect. Jumps that soar through the air must get to the required pose in flight, arresting, as it were, the pose in a dynamic momentary "stop-action," so the eyes of the beholder clearly see the finished product. Viewers are not much interested in how the jumper gets to the pose. They do not care about the process, only the result. If the arms and legs are always on the move from one position to another, then the eyes only see a blur of movement, a fuzzy process that transitions through positions. There are some exceptions, but most jumps should be executed *in* the given pose, not *to* the pose. And there is almost always a "quiet" moment in the air (usually the apex of the jump) when the jump is most easily and best appreciated by viewers. This important aspect of good classical ballet dancing (and training) is grossly neglected, but it is not the fault of students who struggle to overcome gravity. The onus is on teachers. Take care of business!

Regardless of a step's jumping dynamics—pose, position, etc.—the preparatory step(s) must place the dancer in a balanced (TBS) position precisely at the moment of the takeoff, whether it is a takeoff from one or two legs. This means that the dancer should (theoretically) be able to stop the jump at the moment of takeoff and be in complete balance (control). Likewise, there should be complete balance (control) when the jump is concluded. The dancer should be able to hold the landing pose instead of running out of it to recover his balance prior to continuing on with another movement.

And, most important, observers should be able to clearly discern the proper alignment of body parts required by TBS, whether it is a wide lunging fourth position or a simple fifth position. This process of control is what makes viewing dance aesthetically appealing, where everything looks "right" during each phase of correctly executed movements.

Many small jumps travel only incidentally and are therefore easier to control. Most big jumps have a larger traveling component. However, only a scant handful of these are primarily "distance" jumps. The majority of grand allegro steps are designed to be high soaring leaps that also travel—not vice versa. Therefore, in the learning process, teachers must be familiar with each jump's dynamic requirements and teach their students the correct emphasis.

A final obvious demand: All jumps require coordination. However, coordination is especially challenged by the dynamics of jumping. To achieve effective big jumps, there must be a complete coordination of the arms and legs, and the body must be in just the right place at the right time. This means that the arms and legs must get to their required positions in the most efficient way possible. Other circuitous routes will not only rob power from the leap but also likely arrive too late (or too early) to effectively assist the jump.

For example, it is common for a grand allegro step such as jeté entrelacé to take off from a wide lunging fourth position followed by a gathering of all of the power sources into a single vertical takeoff effort from the floor while flying to the desired ending pose. The required traveling ingredient of the jump is almost entirely provided by the preparatory steps that precede the takeoff. There are four essential vertical elevation providers (not listed in sequential order):

1. The grand battement of the leading leg that starts the jump.
2. Raising the arms from the preparatory pose through first position to third position.
3. A powerful push off the floor from the supporting leg.
4. Other ingredients include inhaling, lifting the chest and head vertically, and feeling the "upness" of the jump.

All of the foregoing elements must happen simultaneously or in the proper sequence. If one is left out or is late (or early), then the jump will be prejudiced to some extent. Each element has its vital role to play. It is all too common to observe dancers who have not been taught these imperatives. Therefore, it is incumbent on teachers to understand them and make sure that their young leapers grow into a knowledge of how to perform their jumps efficiently and effectively and not just superficially. Dancers with weak jumps are usually boring dancers. Don't let this happen to your students.

CHAPTER 10

Turning Imperatives

*Art comes to you proposing frankly to give
nothing but the highest qualities to your
moments as they pass.*

Walter Pater

The audience's enjoyment of classical ballet performances is, to a great extent, fed by a dazzling display of turns of all sizes and shapes, each of which seems impossible to most viewers. Turns are done while standing on one or both legs on the floor, and they are also done in the air. They can be done in a variety of poses, from compact to wide open. They can end in simple small poses or in more dynamic large poses. They can conclude a series of movements, or they can begin a combination, and every other possibility in between. They can travel along the diagonal or around a circle or be done in place. And they are capable of astounding the audience with a seemingly impossible number of consecutive repetitions.

During the early years of ballet training, elementary students learn simple half and full turns on both legs, at first done at the barre. Later, these simple turns are done in the center. They are followed by turns on one leg (pirouettes or tours sur le cou-de-pied), first one at a time, later in greater numbers and in a variety of poses and positions.

Today's audiences expect to see dancers performing multiple pirouettes—the more the merrier, it seems. In addition to turns executed by individual dancers, there are also turns by ballerinas who are supported by their partners. These may be pirouettes as well as promenades (tours lents) in various poses.

There are also myriad turns that take place exclusively in the air—fast ones, slow ones, double ones, high ones, long ones, and all-akimbo ones. Turns are fun to do and fun to watch. They comprise the special family of movements that audiences love to see, because they seem impossible to "civilians."

The audience loves them, because everyone knows that you get dizzy when you spin. There are all sorts of children's games that entice boys and girls to spin until they get dizzy. Sometimes children just spin so that they can make themselves dizzy and then stagger around until their equilibrium returns. However, ballet students, as a part of submitting themselves to the regimen of learning how to dance, are taught that being dizzy leads to a loss of control with undesirable consequences. Therefore, they learn spotting techniques to avoid such disorienting moments.

The technique of learning how to spot should be taught to elementary students. Learning this fundamental early on will equip them to later tackle the challenges of learning how to turn without fear and getting disoriented. This is first done by just spinning around oneself in the center of the room. It is done on the whole foot in a shuffling motion (turning by stepping from one foot to the other in rapid succession) with the feet in a loosely turned-out fifth position. The eyes must remain precisely focused straight forward at eye level while the head and rest of the body maintain TBS.

While turning to the right (clockwise), the body turns in a coordinated and collected manner. The head remains facing front as long as possible with eyes looking at a precise "spot" on the wall. Begin turning with the right foot in front, shuffling in this position until the eyes are looking over the left shoulder. Then, without stopping the body's rotation, the head immediately moves to the right shoulder with the eyes returning to the same "spot" that they were previously looking at a moment earlier.

Repeat this exercise several times in a row with precise musical phrasing (in the beginning, do each turn in four counts). Without stopping the shuffling steps, during the first two counts, begin turning with the head remaining front and the eyes focused on the "spot." Change the head to the opposite shoulder between counts two and three. Keep eyes focused on the "spot" while returning to the original starting place on count four. It should almost feel as though the eyes never left the "spot." (This is critical!) While turning clockwise, repeat several times. Stop and repeat everything turning counterclockwise.

Once introduced, this exercise should be done in every lesson until there is no residual dizziness or disorientation after a series of turns and the spotting mechanics are precise. The above turning exercise should then be complicated as follows:

1. Speed up the tempo while maintaining a four-count turn.
2. Execute the shuffling footwork on demi-pointe in fifth position.
3. Speed up the footwork and do each turn in two counts.

It is imperative that the head remain vertical throughout the series of turns. It should never tilt but pivot around its own axis (continuation of the spine through the back of the neck).

Now that we have laid the groundwork for turns with the basic fundamentals of TBS and "spotting," we can proceed to the more complex theories of coordinated rotations of all types.

Just as arabesque is probably the most familiar pose in classical ballet, there is probably no movement more closely identified with classical ballet than the pirouette. It is safe to say that pirouettes can be seen in nearly every ballet ever choreographed, from the Romantic era in the mid-nineteenth century; through the classic era of Petipa; until today, when we have many contemporary balletic styles, including those that are sometimes influenced by jazz and modern dance.

Every classical ballet methodology and school places a strong emphasis on students' turning ability. Let's find out how they tick. First we must reiterate that perfecting pirouettes requires mastery of the basic stance. The ability to perform multiple pirouettes is based on TBS. Without proper alignment, it is nearly impossible to execute more than two or three pirouettes before losing control. This means that students who do not (or cannot) control their basic stance are doomed to a career of iffy pirouettes. If they manage to obtain professional dancer status, they will constantly worry when they attempt to perform turns required by the choreography. Every professional dancer knows that there is no worse feeling than to have to perform steps that one cannot do with confidence. Let's make sure that our students are good turners.

The aforementioned exercise, whereby students spot as they spin around themselves, combined with other useful half and full turning exercises on two legs, both at the barre and in the center, will prepare us for this great milestone. Readers are directed to Vera Kostrovitskaya's book, which carefully outlines the step-by-step procedures. Preparations for pirouettes should be introduced first at the barre and only in the center after they are assimilated. If these preparations are rigorously adhered to, the result will be consistent and dependable turns. Everyone's goal.

The positions of the feet that pirouettes most commonly originate from are second, fourth, and fifth. Each has its own unique challenges. However, they all have certain things in common, which are again based on the basic stance. More than any other step, turning movements cannot be mastered without proper alignment. There is just too much happening while the body is spinning, beginning with the all important relevé from the preparatory starting position.

Nearly all pirouettes begin with a relevé out of plié that transfers the weight from two feet onto one. The relevé should not be a soft or gradual rise onto demi-pointe. Although measured, it must be an aggressive vertical spring. The relevé move is immediately followed by the placement of the arms, working foot and leg in the desired pose. Then follow a rhythmic spotting of the head for the required number of turns as the body spins; the proper amount of rotating force to accomplish the number of intended turns; and finally a controlled finish in the final pose. It sounds complicated. It is. But it can be made simpler by following some important rules applicable to pirouettes on demi-pointe. (Rules for pirouettes on pointe are analogous).

RELEVÉ

No other pirouette ingredient is more important than the relevé. Without an accurate relevé the pirouette is doomed. Regardless of from which foot position on the floor the student begins, the relevé must rise up energetically to a maximum demi-pointe. Anything less than a fully raised demi-pointe results in a weakened position that most likely will not be able to sustain a rock-solid turning position. When balancing in this position the arched instep of the supporting foot should be clearly visible. A partially stretched foot is unacceptable and creates a weak foundation platform on which to turn.

It is also clearly evident that a relevé that does not rise straight up may send the body upward but slightly off the vertical plumb line, resulting in a "leaning" relevé that can only sustain a short-lived balance. Also, remember the imperative of pressing the toes against the floor while balancing on the ball of the foot. They provide a consistent stable mini-platform on which to balance and turn.

CORE ROTATION

All pirouettes are the result of turns that commence from the spring off of the floor. Naturally, everything rotates in unison to initiate the turn. However, the heaviest single portion of the body is the torso, and torso rotation is the most neglected aspect of mastering pirouettes. Having already established the foundation of a correct basic stance, where all body parts are connected to each other and vertically aligned in the most efficient manner, in order to turn with complete control, we have to spin the torso that "sits" on top of the legs which are being forced upward via the relevé.

Torso spin happens simultaneously with the relevé. No single body part or area of the torso should spin faster than any other. This means that the torso turns as a collection of unified body parts, i.e., hips directly below corresponding shoulders, and with back and stomach muscles holding everything together. In addition, the rib cage must not be allowed to "flare" up or out. This is accomplished by engaging the abdominal muscles by having them "reach" upward and grab on to the rib cage, while simultaneously tightening the tops of the buttock muscles (glutei maximi) to keep the pelvis level. These actions, working in unison, maintain core alignment that is essential for mastering turns of all kinds as well as all poses and jumps.

Important note: Under no circumstances should the buttocks be pushed or tucked under. Although a commonly heard admonition, "tucking under" allows the stomach, rib cage and back to be relaxed as the buttocks is pushed under the pelvis. While it is true that tucking under might initially help to align the pelvis, this action induces a "soft" alignment, not one based on strength. In addition, other undesirable reactions can creep into the picture. The hips can be forced forward of their proper alignment, and the thighs, knees, etc., can remain relaxed. The dancer might look aligned to the untrained eye, but he or she is not in a state of readiness prepared to attack any technical challenge.

ARMS

The arms play a secondary, but vital, role in performing good pirouettes. Contrary to some popular opinions, they do *not* provide primary turning force for pirouettes. Their main function is to gather into a predetermined position while at the same time helping the turner to balance. If one studies good natural turners a keen eye can detect some almost imperceptible adjusting movements that allow the turner to do mid-pirouette repair work. This ability is rarely learned. It is usually a facility that natural turners evolve into subconsciously. I have found that even those who possess this ability cannot explain it or teach it. These remarkable turners are able to correct failing balances during pirouettes and continue turning, while most of the rest of us humans must finish our turns and try to salvage a decent ending.

The arms should not be used to provide major rotating force, even in the beginning of the turn. For example: One can readily see that if the leading arm opens sharply and gets ahead of the body in its zeal to provide force, it must, at some point during the turn, slow down and/or move in the opposite direction to collect itself into its proper turning position, thus, in effect, nullifying the force that it initially provided. Also, the closing arm should not race to its turning position in order to provide force independently of its connection to the corresponding shoulder and torso. That is to say, the proper way to use the closing arm is to bring it energetically to its turning position while also remaining well connected to its corresponding shoulder (and hip). By using the arms in this way, they contribute to the torso's more aggressive turning energy, but do not overpower it or sluggishly weigh it down.

An element of providing turning force with the arms is often neglected, especially with pirouettes en dehors, when the arms during the preparation are often in an allongé (outstretched) position. With the front arm in first position and side arm in second position, both arms must begin at the same height as in their turning positions, so that no height adjustment is necessary during the initial phase of the turn.

During the relevé, when the arms begin to close from their allongé positions to a normal rounded first position, the second position arm must "motivate" the lateral rotation of its corresponding shoulder in the direction of the pirouette and go after the raised working knee. Therefore, for example, when executing an en dehors pirouette to the right, the closing left arm motivates the left shoulder to energetically "pursue" the raised working right knee, while at the same time, the right knee "chases" after the rotating left shoulder, thus imparting a coordinated spin to the right of these two key body parts. Naturally, it is assumed that all other related elements of the pirouette are correctly applied, i.e., high demi-pointe; strongly held high working knee; and energetically pulled-up basic stance.

Simultaneously, the first position (allongé) arm joins the other arm while changing into the rounded position. The aggressive closing from the allongé position of the first position arm will force the corresponding elbow slightly outward toward the direction of the turn while pushing against the shoulder. Try to visualize and internalize these instructions. They will help to instill good coordination habits for dependable multiple pirouettes.

LEGS

The legs play an obviously important role in all turns, especially turns on the floor such as pirouettes. We have already discussed the importance of the relevé. Therefore, I will not reiterate details of that aspect of the legs' participation, except to say that students must give special emphasis to strengthening the legs and feet in order to rise to a strong, stable, and sustainable demi-pointe position.

In this section I have been limiting my description of pirouettes to the technique for doing them on demi-pointe. The technique for pirouettes on full pointe is analogous. I shall only say that, since there is less of the foot (toes only) in contact with the floor while wearing pointe shoes, there is less friction that tends to slow down the turn. A good turner should, therefore, be able to execute more pirouettes on pointe than on demi-pointe.

In the Vaganova methodology the rise to demi-pointe is accomplished by a spring from demi-plié from the heels upward onto the balls of the feet. (The so-called "roll-up" method is not used.) The spring from plié accomplishes two important things—an energetic rise onto demi-pointe of the supporting leg combined with a simultaneous placing of the working foot and leg into their turning positions.

Elementary students should begin learning pirouettes sur le cou-de-pied with the working foot placed in a somewhat high conditional cou-de-pied position (in front of and approximately midway between the ankle and the knee). Later on, the working foot position can be raised so that the little toe touches the supporting leg just below the kneecap. Although the beginner foot position is fairly low, it is useful for elementary students to learn pirouette basics with this placement—at first. Later, students will find their own "best" individual turning position. Under no circumstances can the working leg's ankle be allowed to cross over the supporting leg.

It goes without saying that both legs must be well turned out. While executing pirouettes en dehors, the outward rotation (away from the supporting leg) of the turn encourages the turnout of the supporting leg. In addition, the thigh of the raised working leg, while helping to maintain the height of the working foot on the supporting leg, must also be strongly turned out as it helps to lead the rotating torso in the direction of the turn. However, this does not mean that it is the responsibility of the working leg's knee to pull the pirouette around.

Just the contrary is required while executing pirouettes en dedans. A common error in turning en dedans (inward toward the supporting leg), is that the working leg provides too much lateral force in the direction of the turn and gets ahead of the spinning torso. When this happens the torso gets lazy; the supporting leg turns in; and the working leg gets ahead of the hips and winds up providing the majority of turning force instead of being a collaborator.

It is imperative that the torso always provide the primary rotational force for all turning movements both on the floor and in the air. This rule applies to both vertical and inclined rotating steps. In the case of pirouettes, the vertically held torso-block is pushed upward from below by the rise to demi-pointe, while the arms gather into their designated turning positions. The energetically turned-out working leg maintains a subtle steady pressure in the direction of the turn. However, the turnout of the working leg must not independently push against the hips, because this would cause a reaction of the shoulders in the opposite direction (away from the turning direction).

At first, this use of the working leg might feel strange to the novice, especially when trying to execute en dedans turns. This is because it feels as if he is holding the working leg back away from the turning direction. However, once the rotation has begun and all body parts are in their proper positions, turning out against the rotation does not nullify rotational energy. This is because the working leg has nothing to push against. Everything is spinning in a collected manner in the direction of the turn.

To summarize, all body parts must feel a unified steady pressure in the direction of rotation. Nothing remains idle. Nothing rests. The entire body is in a state of connected active readiness, and everything collaborates in providing the appropriate rotational energy—including the mind. But, more about this later.

FOOT

We have previously touched on the mini-platform a high demi-pointe creates when the weight is evenly distributed over the ball of the supporting foot with each of the five toes pressed into the floor. Merely allowing the toes to just rest on the floor makes the challenge of balancing dependent on trying to support the entire body on the ball of the foot alone. The ball needs help from its attached appendages. In their own small way, the toes play a vital roll in controlling balance.

In summary, secure pirouettes require an aggressively spinning torso with arms gathering into their pose, while simultaneously applying connected steady pressure of all body parts in the turning direction. And everything must be combined with the aforementioned imperatives for legs and feet. Combined, all of the above contribute rotational energy to the spinning body. It must be mentioned that, while the head rotates, its main function is spotting to maintain equilibrium, not additional turning force. This is because the head lags behind the turn in the beginning and only turns to catch up just before the body return back to the front.

The foregoing makes it clear that coordinating repeatable secure pirouettes can be a daunting challenge. Indeed, it is for most students in the beginning. However, the process can be made somewhat easier when one realizes that a dancer who is preparing to attack any movement is more than likely only able to focus on a single thought before launching forth. For pirouettes this key thought must be on elements of the relevé. Everything else can fit into its proper place if the relevé is done strongly and accurately. Therefore, the dancer must only focus on an absolutely vertical relevé on the supporting leg that leads the way to demi-pointe. On the contrary, even if everything else is executed perfectly, the pirouette will fail if the relevé is not done with exactitude.

Readers—visualize the foregoing well. Try to internalize these instructions and "feel" what has been described. It is key to doing consistently dependable pirouettes.

CHAPTER 11   *The Poses of Classical Ballet*

Be still within in even the most vibrant activity.
Be vibrantly alive in the midst of every pose.

Indira Gandhi

The mastery of classical ballet technique is based on the mastery of poses, of which there are myriad. While some are static, others are connected to auxiliary movements that help one pose flow smoothly to another. The eye of the beholder attempts to arrest these poses, or fix them, as they transition from one to the other. This is how untutored eyes are able to appreciate the artistic "pictures" that are revealed by the performer. However, if viewers only see transitions without being able to consider the finished product (pose), then they are left with unfulfilled expectations. They may not be able to put their finger on the problem, but they sense that something is missing.

Poses represent the culmination of preparatory actions designed to create an image in the eye of the beholder. When a pose has been created, all actions must pause, so that the viewer can take in the finished product. However, the pose continues to have a life. It breathes. Whether a pose is a "stop-action" or part of a transitioning movement, it must breathe. It is a living thing. It is never just an object to admire, no matter how beautiful on the surface.

Sculptures, drawings, and paintings by great artists capture the essence of the subject even as their work captures life at a static moment. When viewing such works of art, one senses the life of the object. They evoke a message. The same principles apply to classical dance.

In classical ballet certain poses are seen more often than others. For example, a ballerina's pose in first arabesque on pointe is possibly the most commonly seen of all. Examples of this pose can be seen in nearly every magazine, in every program, in every classroom, and in every choreographer's repertory of steps. Because first arabesque is a revealing pose to study, photos of it are often required material to be included in audition résumés by job-seeking hopefuls. It tells a great deal about the proportions of a dancer's body, her sense of "line," her extension, her turnout, her placement, and her expressivity. The same criteria apply to male dancers.

However, what most knowledgeable viewers—including company directors, choreographers, and ballet masters—want to see is a spark of life within the image of the pose, even when it is presented as a stop-action photo. Likewise during performances, viewers are eager to feel the same life that poses evoke as dancers move from one to another. While most audience members are not sophisticated enough to detect precise artistic qualities in any given pose, they can usually feel the warmth and vibrancy of artistically done poses.

Discussing a specific pose such as first arabesque is much easier than contemplating movements that transition quickly from position to position or from one pose to another. Nevertheless, each movement has its unique moment when the step is most clearly perceived by the viewer. It may only be an instant, but it is that precise moment when the movement (pose or position) most clearly registers in the viewer's mind. It is imperative that teachers know when that exact moment should take place, so that they can communicate to their students this important aspect of learning the art of dance. For students, this has very little to do with learning the ins and outs of mere technique, even at the virtuoso level. It is a concept of stagecraft and is essential to the art of dance. All good choreography illustrates and relies on this concept.

Abstract ballet has a more onerous task in establishing the artistic quality of poses and movements. This is because there is usually little or no characterization required by the dancer performing the work. Since the dancer is not required to create a persona onstage, specific human traits are often not called for or even desired by choreographers. Nevertheless, emotions can be injected into abstract movements that register strongly with viewers, such as intensity, passion, envy, strength, weakness, joy, and sadness.

Great artists are able to find within themselves the precise ingredient that clearly differentiates one emotion from another while executing a certain pose. Lesser performers might do the steps well, but they lack the subtleties that turn ordinary movements into memorable art.

In story ballets the task is somewhat easier because the performers are able to lean on their perceptions of the characters they are portraying. There is a story line. There are interactions with other characters that stimulate certain actions and reactions. This happens even in fantasy ballets like *Swan Lake,* in which a bird interacts with a man. Choreographers of such ballets must stretch their imaginations to direct their dancers to the desired interpretation. Meanwhile, the dancers must also use their imaginations accordingly to convince viewers that what they do is authentic and pertinent to the choreographer's intention.

In the case of *Swan Lake,* for example, a ballerina portraying the White Swan must somehow combine human characteristics and feelings with her interpretations of how a swan in distress might move or respond. This situation is further complicated when the same ballerina must also portray the qualities and personality of her own counterpart, the Black Swan, who exhibits altogether different characteristics. It is this blending of qualities that differentiates one ballerina from another and makes *Swan Lake* a great classic that will live forever in ballet history.

Meanwhile, poses and certain movements that are appropriate for *Swan Lake,* regardless of how beautiful, are inappropriate for other ballets that establish their identity through other criteria. For example, the utter humanity expressed in the choreography of *Romeo and Juliet* demands another approach to many of the same poses found in *Swan Lake.* This also applies to Balanchine's *Serenade* or Fokine's *Les Sylphides.* The reason why these (and other) great ballets are considered to be masterpieces is that they were created with uniquely identified qualities that do not cross over into other works, even though they use similar technical ingredients.

One must also differentiate between poses that can be considered primary or secondary in their usage and interpretation. In one ballet a pose could be choreographed to make a strong specific statement, whereas in another ballet the same pose might be used to merely connect other movements. A pose might be key to the choreographic image (primary). The same pose might only be an incidental (secondary) contributor to create a totally different overall impression.

How do performers differentiate between portrayals and interpretations?

Life itself is the best guide. In this regard students and young dancers often lack life experiences that they can draw on to express profound feelings. Of course, the choreographer will have his or her own ideas. But sometimes choreographers are not specific and wait to see what their dancers are able to bring to the table.

Some choreographers ask their dancers for input, while others know exactly what they want. Therefore, it is integral to the art of dance that dancers expand their own imaginations. This is especially important when performers are asked to portray emotions that they have never personally experienced. Without other guidelines to follow, artists must use their imaginations to reveal the desired effect. All of these aspects play into the proper scheme of using poses to illustrate the many possibilities of feelings and emotions. They play a critical role in expressing the art of dance.

The arms and hands also provide a unique sculptural composition to every pose and movement. They can even contribute to the emotional content of the desired pose when the mere execution of dance steps is raised to the level of art. Therefore, the arms and hands always add a dimension of expressiveness to the steps being performed.

Finally, the eyes, being the "windows of the soul," provide the ultimate nuance of expressiveness to every pose. The eyes betray emotions, whether one is happy or sad, angry or bewildered, passionate or passive. How can a dancer portray such emotions convincingly with a bland, unchanging expression? From the very beginning young students should be taught the importance of showing self-confidence, even as they struggle with challenges. In addition to being an essential element of every pose, self-confidence is a vital component of stagecraft.

Most students have trouble showing expressiveness in their dancing, because they are usually preoccupied with the execution of steps. However, they must be taught that movement without feeling is lifeless and little more than stylized calisthenics.

CHAPTER 12 *Advice to Students*

*The dancer who neglects the artistic nuances
during class can rarely—if ever—display true
artistry during performances.*

Alexander Gorsky

The pathway to perfection is an arduous climb. It is often obscure and rife with misleading indicators. Climbers find the path less difficult when they keep the high goal always before them (in sight) instead of pondering the difficulty of the journey and counting their footsteps along the way. The expectation of positive results turns the labor into joyous expectation and speeds progress. However, since perfection is unattainable, anyone who expects perfection will always be disappointed and feel frustrated.

When difficulties seem to overwhelm and discouragement sets in, it is time to reevaluate expectations. Are they realistic? Do you expect too much? Is achievement proportionate to the required labor? Are your motives fame or personal gratification? Is this activity something that you really *need* to do? Or are you doing it because it has become a habit?

Dancers must be realistic. They are engaged in a warfare with what the human body claims are limitations and with what the human mind claims to be artistic insensitivities. How hard are you willing to work to overcome these seemingly insurmountable obstacles?

The human mind often bulldozes its way forward in spite of obstacles and indicators that we are on the wrong path, even when the effort produces no progress. It is important to understand that it is often the "quiet" mind that becomes more alert to the unimpeded pathway, thus avoiding boulders that would block the way. For example, it is not always a different teacher or a new school that opens the way forward but alert awareness of the value of information and guidance already received. And you must learn how to conquer your own self-imposed demons before you can recognize the right path that leads to your goal.

Sometimes you find yourself standing at a crossroad. In spite of indicator signs, you opt to travel in a direction that seems more tempting than the one your instincts tell you is right. You should not be surprised when you arrive at a brick wall with no door to the other side or ladder to climb over.

At other times, at a similar crossroad, you become confused because there are no signs to guide you. However, you have a strong feeling that one path is the right one, even though the way seems strewn with obstacles. What should you do?

Proven pedagogic methodologies map out the path for subsequent generations of students. Rise to the challenge of learning lessons already proven by others. Do not dare to judge. You do not yet have enough experience to entertain such critical opinions. Sometimes lessons are learned slowly, but this is not the fault of the method. Attainment of high goals is usually accompanied by doubts and defeats and triumphs.

Never blame others for your inability (or unwillingness) to follow the path. Always search your own perspective first. Clean house. Get rid of mental garbage. This process is everyone's individual responsibility in artistic pursuits, as in all aspects of life. Ponder your chosen path. Do not judge, criticize, or condemn others. Don't justify your mistakes. And do not envy the successes of others, even when you think it is undeserved.

Serious ballet study not only teaches you how to be a good dancer. It also teaches you poise, posture, etiquette, discipline, thoughtfulness, control, and other life lessons. Classical dance study also aids jazz, modern, and tap dancers. It is an essential building block. Numerous athletes have also benefited. And ballet classes are a good place for anyone to improve their outlook on life, where striving for successes and dealing with failures are commonplace.

Not everyone has a special talent or the ability to accomplish something important. Most people are wearied by their work, especially if it is a strenuous task they confront. However, they can take pride in their labors and possibly use their talents to become the best at whatever it is that they enlist to do. Such workers are deserving of praise and rewards. The great Spanish cello virtuoso Pablo Casals once said, "Do not waste life and love in things you do not feel. Do what you feel and listen to your conscience. If you do that, you will do right for the world and for yourselves."

Whatever you choose to do, do it with conviction. Every student must grapple with expectations. Are they realistic? Test yourself by honestly answering the following questions:

1. Are you willing to set aside every distraction in the honest and realistic pursuit of your dreams?
2. Are you willing to work, work, and work to achieve your goal?
3. Do you know how to work? Or are you just a dreamer?
4. Do you blame others for your inability to achieve goals? Are you willing to change your attitudes and beliefs?
5. Do you think that you know more than your teachers?

A true dance artist must fully comprehend the simplicity, refinement, and infinite variety of his art. The dancer is not in the dance. Dance is in the dancer. Otherwise, dance would command all movement, and the dancer would be powerless.

Never be impressed by foolish flattery. Be a realist, and be honest with yourself. The human mind is a powerful tool. Use it! Exploit it! Plumb the depths of its potential. However, you must learn to discriminate between self-serving human will and inspired revelation. How can you discern the difference? True progress is attained when technical execution and artistic expression become one—each complementing the other and neither standing apart waving its own red flag.

Constantly evaluate the objects you pursue and what you expend your energy on. Are they worthy? Or just personal glorification? Analyze objectives to see if they are worthy goals. Do they contribute to the art or just make you happy (proud)? The goals you choose to pursue and the attitudes you manifest in this quest are revealing. Let the perfect model be always present in your thought. Anything else shuts out the possibility of revelation and inhibits progress.

Commit yourself to success. It takes guts to set goals. Most people are afraid to set goals because they are afraid of failure. However, great artists begin their journey with high goals before them. These goals may seem far off in the beginning, and progress may be excruciatingly slow, but even slow progress does not discourage committed students.

Write down your goals, but be realistic. Talk about your aspirations with like-minded friends or family and your teacher. This step holds you accountable, especially when you are tempted to give up. Those with whom you shared your ideas will undoubtedly encourage you through the hard times. When you commit yourself in this way you open windows of opportunity. You are more apt to actively take the necessary steps to continue the journey. Be consistent and focused on this course.

Be wise in making decisions that impact on your goals. Be committed. Enjoy the process and whatever it brings. Do not postpone actions that help you confront inevitable challenges. And remember, life is not a dress rehearsal. Whatever happens today rapidly becomes ancient history. Therefore, take advantage of every opportunity to work toward your goal.

Do not be afraid to take risks. Careful dancers are boring dancers, and class is the best place to test yourself. Dancers who dance small for fear of showing weaknesses or perceived inadequacies are uninteresting and never attract much attention. For committed dancers, any mistake becomes a big blunder because they attack boldly, come what may. Then they learn from that experience so as not to repeat the error.

In class, never dismiss a correction as unnecessary or not applicable to you, whether it is given to you or to another student. Every correction is an opportunity to leap over another obstacle. And do not expect the same correction to be given to you repeatedly. Hear it once, and heed the admonition. Then put the guidance to work.

No matter how daunting, enjoy the process. No matter how demanding, rise to the challenge. When things seem to go badly, it is usually the human mind that resists and gets us into trouble. Take charge of your thoughts and your destiny.

CHAPTER 13

General Instructions to Pupils

> *Man in his highest development approaches*
> *the child. If an adult is a good person, in his*
> *heart he is still a child. In every person, the best,*
> *the most important part is that which remains*
> *from his childhood.*
>
> George Balanchine

In 1820, at the age of seventeen, Carlo Blasis published *An Elementary Treatise upon the Theory and Practice of the Art of Dancing*. Blasis's amazingly profound insights as a teenager are unprecedented. He went on to a long and illustrious career in the theater as a dancer, teacher, director, choreographer, and writer and died in 1878. His theories inspired the great master teacher Enrico Cecchetti to continue the tradition of classical ballet, Italian style. Years later Cecchetti in turn inspired Agrippina Vaganova to create her own unique syllabus for classical ballet instruction, which still influences teachers around the world more than fifty years following her death.

Blasis's advice to students is translated by Mary Stewart Evans:

> To you young people who are about to take up dancing as a career and are earnestly resolved to persevere and achieve success, my first advice is to put yourself into the hands of an experienced master. It is impossible to be too careful in your choice, as by no means have all teachers had a sound training and very few have distinguished themselves as executants. Theory alone does not suffice for the exact demonstrations of the principles of dancing. And far from augmenting the number of

good dancers, mediocre instruction reduces it, as everything depends upon the elementary grounding. A bad habit once acquired is almost impossible to eradicate. Even among good teachers there are those with a mania for innovation who claim that their methods are a constructive contribution to the true precepts of the art, while in reality they serve only to destroy them.

You will need plenty of courage and tenacity of purpose. Practice regularly every day, and remember that frequent interruption hinders progress and is a loss never regained. On the other hand, excessive work is injurious and may even be prejudicial to health. Be moderate in all things, including your pleasures, and beware of exercises other than dancing. For example, fencing, riding, running, etc., are all forms of exercise harmful to a dancer. Terpsichore [the Greek muse who presides over dance] is a stern goddess and demands complete sacrifice. Hers is not an easy path, and you will find many obstacles to surmount. Though you be gifted at birth with the beauty and perfection of form of an Apollo, and every other aspect be ideal, you will never attain success without hard work and intelligent study under a good master. Unceasing endeavor is the price of real ability, and even the mature dancer must practice constantly.

You should spare no effort to acquire steadiness and perfect equilibrium. While upon the stage, the dancer should never cease to be a potential model to painter or sculptor, and this aim may well represent the summit of his aspiration. The great artist M. Gardel, at the end of an academic discussion on dancing, told me that to judge a good dancer the eye should arrest him, as it were, in mid-air; and if he is found placed in accordance with correct principles, his body presenting a harmonious ensemble worthy of an artist's pencil, then it may be said he has succeeded and deserves to triumph. By this observation M. Gardel shows how deep is his knowledge and how difficult the art of dancing.

The natural ease and facility of your general execution will bear testimony to the mastery you have attained, as the acme of art lies in its concealment. Once you have reached this degree of perfection, universal approbation and the repute of a great artist will be yours. Riccoboni, in his *Representative Art,* says, "Nothing is more dangerous to art than to permit the spectator to penetrate its simulation," and this is an excellent precept for all dancers.

Keen observation and an analytical mind can be of great service to you. Do not scorn any opinion, as occasionally even a poor dancer has certain good points by which you could profit. You should not be afraid to ask your master questions and to discuss your art freely with him. Do not be ashamed if you make mistakes, but benefit by his corrections and put his counsel into practice at once to impress it upon your mind.

Worship beauty and never deviate from the true principles of your art. Above all do not allow the temporary success of a few bad dancers, who please a blind public by their acrobatic antics and ridiculous pirouettes, to lead you into emulating their errors. The triumph of these worthless artists is of short duration. Truth and sincerity will find them out in the end.

A dancer of talent should have nothing but contempt for the flattery that fools lavish upon the charlatan and should concern himself only with the opinion of men of artistic discrimination whose approbation can provide a stimulus to the perfection of his work.

You must learn to discriminate between types. Nothing is in more deplorable taste than a tall stately dancer, suitable for serious roles, dancing the rustic's part in a comic ballet, or more absurd than a short thick-set dancer rigged out as the hero in an adagio. A hero behaving as a jocular country bumpkin would indeed be a ridiculous sight. The famous Greek orator Horace once said, "Each should have his own appearance and his own fame."

Great artists, whether painters, poets, or musicians, have taken care not to confuse the personalities and mannerisms of different characters. They have always adhered to distinction of type, and by following them you will give proof of your own good taste.

Interest yourself in dance composition, seeking novelty in enchaînements, figures, attitudes, and groups. Regard yourself as a painter in composing and assembling, to the end that everything in your picture is harmonious and combines a lifelike animation with alluring grace.

The music must always be in keeping, and it is this delightful ensemble that captures all hearts and charms even the least musical. Undoubtedly the pantomime expresses much, but without the tone and feeling of melodious sound it could not move us so deeply.

I shall end my instructions by advising all young students to study both drawing and music, as these will be of the greatest value to them in their art. As draftsmen they will familiarize themselves with graceful and elegant posture and an easy manner of portrayal; as musicians they will possess a surer touch than others. Their ear will give them mastery of movement and time, and their cadenced steps will be in perfect rhythm with the tune. It will also facilitate composition for those who wish to undertake it and add to its accuracy.

CHAPTER 14 *Practice Makes Perfect*

Perfection should never be a fixed goal.
It is a process that requires a realistic attitude
demanding no less than everything.

A. Sage

Practicing and rehearsing are acts of faith. One day, it seems, you dance perfectly. The next day, when you repeat the same steps, they fall apart. Why? It is because your understanding of how to control the steps is not yet secure. However, you must keep practicing, and then one day, a breakthrough. The steps will be performed flawlessly and effortlessly. These small achievements are what keep us going. They get us through the doldrums. They add yet another beacon of light along the obscure pathway to excellence. Be grateful for them.

This kind of focused, disciplined practice makes learning secure. The resulting security will have nothing to do with yesterday's failure (or success) but will follow naturally, because of having arrived at a new level of understanding.

Discipline is the technique of harnessing your own power and potential to help you progress toward higher goals and achievements. Discipline makes it possible to control talent by allowing you to do what you are supposed to do, even when you don't feel like it. When you have discipline, you are willing to surrender selfishness and ego. It allows you to open doors that permit access to achievements above and beyond the competition. This takes time and focused dedication. Therefore, always seek the truth, not merely superficial approbation and praise. Looking good for the moment is not enough.

Being good should be the goal. And getting there requires discipline and practice.

"Practice makes perfect" is not just a tired cliché or a rote routine. It is a purposefully directed attack on the technical and artistic problems that confront you. It is also a refining process that ultimately leads you from practicing technique to the art of dance. To achieve this goal you must have faith, knowing that your efforts will ultimately be rewarded.

Never focus on how difficult is the climb. And never dwell on failures. Have faith that success is just around the corner. You arrive at this level of faith because of having already experienced previous breakthroughs and by attaining goals. Attaining goals reaffirms that we are on the right track, that we understood and applied the rules that helped us advance. It is important never to swerve from your path even when you are tempted to think that you might be making a mistake. Persevere.

Naturally, students are not alone as they confront these challenges. They must place themselves in the hands of knowledgeable teachers who can help them through the maze of frustrations and momentary failures. Such lapses are inevitable, but working through them is essential. Sometimes we are tempted to believe that a teacher cannot teach us anything new, that we have exhausted their resources. But maybe this is due to our own reluctance to change or refocus our energies. Unless there is little doubt about a teacher's inability to take one further, studying with another teacher will not solve anything. And studying with several teachers at the same time will be even less fruitful.

Different opinions and methods only lead to confusion. Worse yet, differing ideas invite students to judge the competency of their teachers—never a positive position to be in. It is essential to find *the* teacher who can determine what you need. And then you must stick with him or her. Maximum progress is much more likely when students and teachers know each other. Unfortunately, it is not so easy to find the right person.

This gives rise to an important question: Are dancers made by their teachers? The answer is an emphatic no. Dancers make themselves by conscientiously practicing the tenets given to them and not deviating from what they are being taught—assuming, of course, that they are receiving good instruction. Workers, focused on the task at hand, succeed because they follow the correct leadings of their teachers.

Practicing (studying) under a knowledgeable teacher may begin as an act of faith. It may even appear to be a risk to trust a new teacher. But this reliance is essential for progress. Faith may begin with a "show me" attitude. But it must evolve into a more positive reliance on the teacher's knowledge and experience. Then, little by little, breakthroughs will occur, bringing concomitant intuitions that one is on the right track. Such concrete evidence ensures a positive outcome. Whether sudden or gradual, breakthroughs result from consistency and persistence.

To achieve great heights, one can never be satisfied with the immediate rewards of work well done. As one plateau is reached, even more work is required to move on. When we cultivate our abilities in this way and practice persistently, we can begin to claim as our own the talents given to us. They begin to feel natural. They empower us and lead us to ever higher achievements.

Resist the temptation to envy others. And do not resent criticisms, whether warranted or unwarranted. Try to discern what can be garnered from them. And resist the "pigme" (not misspelled) syndrome (i.e., "me, the pig" or "me first"). Practice humility and gratitude. Be generous. The reward for such practice is the joy of experiencing work well done, whether it is a small step of progress or a giant leap forward.

CHAPTER 15 *Discipline*

---

*Finding art within dance and cultivating
the imagination become possible only
through organized effort.*

Asaf Messerer

There is nothing more important in art than discipline. But this is not control that is imposed by outside sources. It is self-imposed obedience toward
the authority of the art involving restraint, regulation, and order. Discipline
stems from a need to learn and excel, even rising to heretofore unattained
heights. And the only way to achieve these high goals is through work. One
cannot rely on talent alone.

One must never be satisfied with momentary approval. When you have
discipline, you are willing to surrender selfishness and ego and short-lived
gains, so that you can open doors allowing access to achievement above and
beyond the competition. This takes time, and there is no shortcut.

In classical dance, possessing correct physical attributes is paramount, especially at the professional level. Without natural physical gifts, no matter
how much innate talent, desire, and passion one has, it is impossible to give
the public the performance that they pay for. Classical ballet is an art, not
merely a craft that anyone can learn with time and effort. Therefore, with the
requisite natural gifts, the craft can be refined into art. The process requires
daily, focused hard work while intelligently pursuing specific goals.

A "natural" artist who does not work will fail. A "natural" artist who does
not learn the intricacies of his craft will fail. A hardworking, conscientious

craftsman has a chance to succeed, but only if natural liabilities are few. In most instances natural liabilities cannot be improved upon:

1. You can't grow four inches.
2. You can't shrink three inches.
3. You can't have high extensions if your body does not permit it.
4. You can't reduce the size of your hips.
5. You can't turn out if your joints do not permit it.
6. You can't become musical if you are unable to hear or feel the music.

Good ballet technique can only be attained through disciplined directed action. All involuntary reactions must be strictly eradicated. During the early learning process, these actions must be consciously worked on. Once habits of proper muscle memory are established, actions then become subconscious. Achieving this level of intuitive dancing demands that students never waste time in looking for the easy way. They realize that fulfilling talent's promise demands disciplined hard work. And they never resent the insistence of this requirement. They instinctively know or quickly learn that the pursuit of excellence has its own rewards. Therefore, they are not intimidated by fear or foolish ignorance. A true dance artist never wastes a single moment in self-pity, discouragement, or distractions.

One reaches the pinnacle of technical and artistic heights by day-to-day persistent toil. Steady, small steps of progress eventually win the day, even though most students are impatient to hurry the process. The laborer is rewarded according to his devotion to the task and also his joyful enthusiasm during the process. He learns that if he does today what others won't, tomorrow he will be able to do what others can't. He learns that if he wants to excel, he will have to deal with the possibility of failure. However, he understands that those who are talented and hard workers usually attain their goals. He also understands that those who lack talent but nevertheless persevere attain goals as well. But without question, he knows that quitters never win.

Teachers must make sure that the discipline of learning is an enjoyable experience for their students—no fun, no concentration; no fun, no anticipation. Every correction in every lesson is a reminder of important details. Dancers who do not pay attention to details are doomed. They must learn to work hard on the "little" things. Details, details, details—each one is worthy of attention. High achievements are not easily won and require selfless devotion to worthy ideals.

Most people can learn how to dance (to a certain degree), especially if they are conscientious and work hard at it. However, becoming a strong technician is not enough if the art is missing. This includes all of the aesthetic ingredients that make dancing onstage meaningful and beautiful. And without beauty our art is lost, even when it is disguised by spectacular technical feats or even hidden in the grotesque. In addition to technique, true artists have a natural soaring spirit. Their bodies seem to sing when they dance.

Today, we have far too many craftsmen—people who have learned the technical knack of dancing. Some are extremely good and never cease to amaze viewers with their prowess. However, artists who create beauty when they dance are few.

People dance for many personal reasons. Professional dancers' main reason for performing should be to express the art they feel within. And this should be at the highest possible level. Audiences who come to be elevated out of prosaic lives deserve nothing but the best. However, if a professional dancer's main reason for dancing is to satisfy his own personal desires, then he is in the wrong business. Remember, professional dance is a form of "show business." The art is to be "shown" at its best to paying audiences who deserve no less. Otherwise, viewers are being cheated. This is one of the serious problems that classical ballet is facing today.

Students should be taught that real dancers are either ordinary or truly great. Why would anyone opt for mediocrity? Therefore, students should be urged by their teachers to choose greatness. They must work to come as close as possible to that goal. As in all art, good ballet must be clear and understandable. Dancers must perform their parts intelligently, not just intellectually. Persistence makes such achievement possible.

The skill of harnessing technical power and artistic potential helps dancers progress toward high achievements and goals. But this is precisely what all true dance artists commit themselves to do, even when they don't feel like it. Experienced dancers sometimes feel indisposed or overwhelmed by personal problems. However, professionals do not allow such influences to affect their performances. They are able to surrender selfishness and ego-centered attitudes when the curtain opens and the orchestra begins to play. They do what they are supposed to do.

Occasionally dancers have their best performances under such circumstances. Focused dedication to the task at hand explains this phenomenon. It goes beyond the immediate demand of their commitment or of seeking audience approval. This is being a professional dancer.

The professional understands that dancing is a way of expressing movement of thought. In the process he shows the beauty of the piece, not personal skill. This is an indispensable unselfish approach to choosing a life in classical ballet. It demands focus, action, and integrity, all working together to achieve goals:

Focus makes value judgments. It prioritizes. It is disciplined and orderly.

Action requires persistent effort. No time can be wasted on trivialities or indecision. One must seize opportunities, and be alert to recognize what is required.

Integrity deals with the daily nitty-gritty of the practical steps necessary to realize a vision. It requires one to be considerate of others.

Working as a team also helps define worthy goals and produces an artistic product worthy of the marketplace. It is a commitment to excellence vs. competition, ethics vs. expediency, fairness vs. favoritism, integrity vs. self-indulgence. Such high achievements are not easily attained and require an unselfish devotion to worthy ideals.

CHAPTER 16 *The Mind*

---

*An artist achieves significance when his
talent is used to engage and illuminate
an aspect of human reality.*

Theodore F. Wolff

As Hercule Poirot, Agatha Christie's famous Belgian detective, often says on
the way to solving his most baffling cases, "I must take time to stimulate the
little gray cells." I cannot emphasize strongly enough that the most important "muscle" to exercise in the study of classical ballet is the one between
the ears. If the brain does not direct every action intelligently and precisely,
the dancer is doomed to a constant struggle of controlling involuntary (and
usually undesirable) reactions.

A successful dancer must have a level of mental toughness that unifies
natural physical gifts with learned skills and artistic qualities. This is what
separates great artists from the average. For most high-achievers, mental
toughness and disciplined conscientiousness are innately "hardwired." Although feeling the pressure of challenges (like all normal people), the great
ones relish and thrive under the pressure of the spotlight. They detest the
feeling of being overwhelmed, and they refuse to succumb to challenges.
When confronted with technical problems, they fight to overcome the difficulty. Defeat is unacceptable to them.

The minds of strong students become as strong as their physical ability.
They expect perfect execution every time they set forth. They are totally
committed to the challenge of the movement—what it is trying to communicate. Then they attempt to express the idea or movement clearly and

boldly. An analogy: You must speak clearly and boldly when trying to communicate something important to someone who is far away.

Few students come to the study of classical ballet with a mind already cultivated for the challenges they inevitably must face. However, occasionally teachers discover students who readily accept the idea that they must concentrate on every detail and focus their attention on everything their teacher says. It should be quite obvious that the attribute of conscientiousness is essential, as there is so much material to be learned and assimilated. However, teachers who have been at this work for more than a few years know that it is unusual to find such focused dedication—a rare treat, indeed.

In every class, even ones containing carefully auditioned students, the majority will prove to be plodders. If the teacher is very fortunate, he or she may discover a single true talent in the group. It is almost too much to expect to have more. However, since most good dancers are plodders to some degree, they can be very useful. Indeed, most corps de ballet dancers are plodders, even in top national companies.

The term *plodder* is not meant to be derogatory. It is not that plodders have no talent; otherwise, they would not have been selected in the first place. It just means that they occasionally have difficulty concentrating on the task at hand and may sometimes come to class unfocused or distracted by other compelling demands or interests. It is also possible that physical limitations inhibit progress. Maybe they struggle with their turnout or balance. Or maybe they just don't work hard enough to improve their jumps or their turns.

Plodders are often students who are happy when they receive a B+ or an A– on a final exam in school or on their report card. They don't understand that earning such grades, although much better than average, means that they did not rise to the level of excellence. Plodders usually do not strive for the highest recognition in any endeavor. They are usually not class valedictorians. They are usually not voted into the honor society. They are rarely Phi Beta Kappa. They are satisfied by doing a good job that is above average and deserves some praise. But there is always something that prevents them from fully utilizing their talent.

Plodders often have difficulty rising to new challenges that take them out of their comfort zone. Music accompaniment that is a little faster or a little slower than they like feels like an imposition. They may consider corrections to be personal criticisms. They resent being pushed hard and rationalize that they are doing their best, even when it is obvious that they are not.

When you tell plodders to pull up higher, they return to their comfort zone as soon as you look away. When you tell them not to hop while attempting to balance on demi-pointe at the barre, they hop anyway, even though they are holding the barre. When you give them an important correction, it does not get internalized and must be repeated, sometimes ad infinitum. Plodders easily find excuses for just about every difficulty, and it is never their fault when things do not go well. Nevertheless, in the hands of good teachers, plodders can be molded into competent dancers who are the backbone of nearly every professional company throughout the world.

Occasionally, plodders change and become first-class dancers, even soloists. Following an epiphany, they sometimes accept their teachers' persistent hounding and rise above their natural instincts. Some teachers have a knack for discovering the "chink" in their protective armor, while others have the patience to persist in digging for evasive possibilities. Such teachers are, no doubt, perceptive, patient, and saintly. Not only can they perceive hidden possibilities but they also see these challenges as worthy of the struggle. All such teachers are to be commended, since there are, no doubt, examples of dance artists who were driven by relentless teachers to live up to their potential.

Natalia Makarova is a notable example of a great dancer whose first teachers saw extraordinary talent in spite of a "take it easy" attitude early on. I hasten to add that she was never a plodder.

Without a doubt, plodders have to be pushed. Otherwise, they will never fulfill their potential. Good teachers recognize the possibilities in spite of apparent problems and find ways to turn the situation around. Great teachers are able to get plodders to rise to the challenge of seemingly insurmountable stumbling blocks and press on with the arduous climb up the mountain of difficulties.

Everyone who has seriously studied the art of classical ballet knows how daunting the myriad confrontations are that one must face down on the way up. All experienced and well-trained teachers understand how difficult are the many tests that confront serious students, knowing that today perhaps the challenges seem impossible. However, we also know that most issues can be overcome, and will be overcome, as long as guidance and an appropriate effort are exerted.

Not long ago I enjoyed a Chinese dinner with friends. As is the usual custom, we received fortune cookies at the end of our meal. I feel that mine is worth repeating here: "When you make a mistake, do not treat yourself as though you were the mistake." On a subsequent return visit to the restaurant, my fortune cookie read, "Dwelling on the negative simply contributes to its power." Oriental wisdom can be enlightening.

In many instances, one can accomplish higher goals by simply deciding to rise above the difficulties. It must be a conscious decision, because natural instincts often compete to discourage the required effort. Negative thoughts would try to convince the struggler that the goal is out of reach, or that it is not worth the effort, or even that it is impossible. However, today's impossibility becomes tomorrow's opportunity to succeed. Serious ballet students confront these challenging quandaries repeatedly during their years of study. Small victories eventually convince them that all things are possible.

Rising to ever higher challenges means that one must believe that success is always possible. Therefore, when a teacher says, "Hold your balance without hopping," it is incumbent on the student to do it, not just think about how difficult the challenge is. Telling a student to complete their relevé to a 100 percent demi-pointe is a reasonable expectation and certainly within the realm of possibility for every student. After all, we are not asking them to do a combination of brisés volés with double beats followed by a diagonal of double jetés entrelacés.

A 100 percent relevé is absolutely essential for executing secure, dependable pirouettes and holding balances. In itself, the relevé is not technically challenging. It is merely the foundation for the challenging balance that follows. If one focuses too intently on the balance, then the execution of the relevé is likely to be faulty. First things first. Relevé 100 percent, and then hold the pose. Do not let the body's protests convince you that something is impossible. No excuses.

Just as important is ending a brilliantly done variation with a rock solid final pose that "commands" viewers to appreciate and audiences to applaud. Even more important is ending a variation (or combination) with an expression of self-assured confidence, even when the effort was disappointingly shaky. This is an essential ingredient of show business. It is an element of stagecraft that all students and dancers must learn. Things do not always turn out as planned. But viewers are not interested in being drawn into a dancer's troubles or in seeing reactions that betray displeasure with what happened. Struggles are inevitable, and showing negative reactions is unacceptable.

The creation of a real dancer is the result of refining the mind and body of an intelligent and willing student—one who is eager to work hard to achieve lofty goals. Michelangelo is reported to have said about his sculpture, "God put figures into the stone. My job is to free them."

The mind is a powerful asset. Use it. Rely on it. Take charge!

CHAPTER 17

Music and Musicality

> *To interrupt the inner link with the musical*
> *theme is to depart from interpretive movement into*
> *mere technique. The musical theme must always*
> *manifest itself as the pupil's artistic, emotional,*
> *conscious feeling for dance, as a vital, fully*
> *conscious choreographic cantilena.*
>
> Nikolai I. Tarasov

Musicality is an aptitude for music, and since music is a component of dance, an understanding of it is a prerequisite for dancers. With appropriate music, the physicality of dance is capable of being raised to the heights of poetry. However, with an overemphasis on technique, dance can just as easily descend to a vulgar display of pyrotechnics.

In the process of developing dance abilities, ballet students must refine their musical taste as well as their musicality. Music and dance are inseparable in the training of dance artists, owing to the fact that dance is nearly always performed to music accompaniment.

Although it would be most advantageous if beginner ballet students were familiar with music, it must be assumed that new students are totally unfamiliar with the intricacies of music, especially classical music. In order to deal with this important issue, some national ballet academies require that ballet students study music in addition to taking their dance lessons. Courses typically include music theory, rhythm, harmony, tempo, and melody. In some schools, students are required to study piano and are expected to play the instrument at least competently. There are enormous benefits to be derived from this approach to dance education. And students who show a musical aptitude will have an advantage over those who struggle to understand it.

In addition to executing step patterns, choreographers usually expect to see some degree of musical interpretations from their dancers. It is impossible to be specific about such a subtle question, however, as each choreographer has a different attitude about the dance-music relationship. The collaboration between the music, choreography, and dancer can be fragile, even tenuous. However, suffice it to say that when all ingredients fit together well, there is a feeling of intangible harmony that is satisfying to the viewer, which is one of the first objectives in choreographing a new work of art.

If ballet students are taught to respect music and to recognize music as an essential creative element of their dancing, then they are in a position to probe their own interpretations of the feelings and emotions that the music stimulates. To be able to dance the music with creativity, to "breathe" the melody, requires mastery of the technique, so that difficulties executing the steps do not inhibit artistic expressiveness. Beginner students are not yet ready to demonstrate mastery of such dance dynamics. Therefore, teachers must move slowly in refining the music education of students.

In the beginning, music accompaniment for ballet classes should use simple regular meters with slow tempos. Best are the 2/4s and 4/4s. Their cadence is even and without subtle variations. These rhythms are the easiest to understand and feel, as students embark on learning the strange new movements.

Teachers must remind themselves that everything that is done in the lesson for new students is mysterious and baffling to them. And for most students it remains like that for a long time. Therefore, to introduce more complex rhythm patterns such as 3/4 and 6/8 meters is not recommended in the beginning, even though such meters are closely associated with dancing. The strong "downbeat" on count 1 in the case of 3/4 and on counts 1 and 4 in the case of 6/8 overpowers the weaker following beats and often impels accents that erroneously emphasize what should be smoothly connected movements.

When students are distracted by trying to figure out the dynamics of music, they are unable to concentrate on the proper execution of the steps they are learning. Ballet teachers with a good music education know that certain movements are best learned utilizing certain meters and tempos, and they also know that there will be a right time to introduce the intricacies of more complex music phrasing.

Teachers who are fans of 3/4 time music should not impose on their students waltzy exercises merely because they like the "feeling" that rhythm induces. Although 3/4 time is very commonly heard in classical music, including many well-known ballets, elementary students do not yet have an ear sophisticated enough to correctly interpret the three-part rhythm as it is applied to the dynamics of the new movements. Learning will take longer than necessary if these guidelines are not adhered to.

In spite of the present trend that favors fast tempos in dance, beginner students need slow rhythm patterns. This is especially important in music used for allegro. Jumps should be introduced in isolation—one at a time—with separate preparations and endings. Combinations of allegro steps should only be introduced when *all* of the fundamentals are being done well and confidently by the students. Careful vigilance and patience are required by the teacher in this regard.

Musicality is learned via the correct coordination of movements with the music. Therefore, there should be a count given for each part of the movement. A simple allegro example follows. For executing changements de pied, using one measure of 4/4 time for a single jump:

1. In fifth position with the right foot front, demi-plié in two counts (one quarter note each);
2. On the "and" between count 2 and count 3, spring off the floor and change the feet in the air;
3. Land in fifth position on count 3 with the right foot in back;
4. Straighten the knees on count 4.

Other jumps are similarly taught. One can readily see that using other meters complicates the phrasing and critical moments of emphasis. Naturally, more advanced students can be taught to overcome such challenges, but it would mean an unnecessary imposition that runs the risk of confusing beginners. Let's keep things simple. There is plenty of time later to test our students.

The choice of musical styles by teachers must be carefully considered. Since classical ballet is an established art, it is appropriate to use classical music for its accompaniment. There is a wide repertoire of published classical music by many outstanding composers that is suitable for the classroom. Live accompaniment is best.

However, I hasten to add that there are many excellent recordings available on the market today. Careful scrutiny is advised in making selections. Choose music that has long bands (not less than 32 or 64 measures, including adagios and grand allegros of up to 128 measures). Music with four-count introductions is highly recommended rather than the commonly played two-chord intro that does not give the listener a clue as to what will be the meter, tempo, or phraseology of the music to follow.

On the stage, choreographers and dancers are subject to the music. They should engage with the composer's intent. However, it should be understood that music in the classroom is the polar opposite, where music is subject to the needs of the teacher and students.

In the classroom it is not up to teachers and students to adjust to the music. The accompanist must therefore adapt appropriate music to the requirements of the exercise. This does not mean that music with a particular quality should be so radically changed that it no longer suits a combination. It just means that the accompanist should select music based on how well it induces movement and contributes to the exercise. The same applies to the choice of a recording.

This might mean slowing down or speeding up a music phrase or retarding one phrase as it transitions into an altogether different one. In that sense the original composer might be turning over in his grave in disgruntled annoyance. Nevertheless, the music needs to conform to the plan for the exercise that the teacher has devised.

We are seeing today many crossovers in dance between classical ballet, modern, and jazz styles. However, the ballet classroom is not the place to use music appropriate for these alternate dance forms. Stick to classical music for classical dance. Reserve music from show tunes, pop, jazz, etc., for other classes where these musical styles are more appropriate.

Also, it is best not to use music for the ballet classroom that comes from well-known classical ballets. In most cases, music composed for or adapted to familiar classical ballets is too closely identified with the ballet in which it is used. There may be some exceptions, but seek out music from less familiar ballets that are no longer or rarely performed.

Elementary classes should use music that is simple and uncomplicated, even naïve. Exercises should be in evenly counted measures usually grouped in multiples of eight (i.e., 16, 32, 64, 128, etc.). More advanced class levels can benefit from more sophisticated music that tests the students' phrasing abilities.

The most valuable accompanists for ballet classrooms are adept at improvisation and/or adapting written music to the demands of the teacher's exercise. Accompanists with this ability are a great asset and contribute invaluable assistance to teachers. Improvisations and adaptations based on familiar themes can be useful, as long as they are not melodies that distract the students as they work through their exercises. And, of course, improvisations must always be appropriate for the dynamics of the combination.

In time, students' musical sensitivity will become increasingly acute, which will allow them to phrase their movements in a more dancerly way. Instead of dogmatically following the musical beats, the students will learn how to demonstrate subtle nuanced phrasing. They will learn how to begin and end movements artistically, while simultaneously executing the movements' accented "demand moments"—in the right way and at the right time in the music. This ability comes later as more and more theatrical expressiveness is injected into movements that have heretofore been done rather mechanically.

Dancers who master this subtle aspect of musicality might depart slightly from the rigidity of precise meter. This does not mean that they are any less musical. It just means that they are learning how to "play" the music with their bodies, just as accomplished musicians do not fall victim to strictly playing the notes written on sheets of music in a metronomic dogmatic fashion. Every accomplished musician and dancer knows that the written note is merely a guideline that leads to artistic expressiveness.

During the process of fitting movement to music, dancers learn that their bodies are instruments that sing the music and not mere slaves to tempo and meter. A static pose should breathe, even as it remains motionless. In learning to do this, students must learn to love music. They must be drawn to it. They must be impelled by it. They must feel a need to move when they hear it. This stimulus is not merely conscious understanding. It is the cultivation of inner creativity that is motivated by the music.

Students' movements should be motivated in natural and organic ways.

It is not enough to just do the right step at the right time, although that is what is expected of the lines of swans as they move in unison in *Swan Lake* or the rows of ghostly wilis in *Giselle*. Even as these corps de ballets scenes conform to precise uniformity, they serve to accompany and highlight the central figures of Giselle or the Swan Queen, who use contrasting gestures to sing the beauty of the same music with complementary movements.

Even though the classroom is a theatrical situation with an imaginary audience (the mirror), students should concentrate on learning their exercises with perfect execution, much like the demands imposed on company corps de ballet members. Individual unique dance expressiveness comes later with experience. First, let's get our students to do the steps well. Later, we can help them feel the artistic qualities that turn steps into dancing and dance into art. In the beginning, it is enough that the students listen to the subtleties of the music's meter, tempo, and phrasing and apply them to the myriad of new and unfamiliar steps.

It also should be remembered that, while dancers onstage are already very familiar with the music and how it motivates the choreography, students in the classroom are hearing the music for the first time as it is applied to new steps and combinations given that day by their teacher. Therefore, the task of fitting movements to music is more challenging for students. In this sense there is a greater onus placed on students than dancers, because students are still in the learning process, even though dancers onstage perform their movements to an audience that has high expectations for a well-executed performance.

The demands of good dancing are very exacting. Dancing precisely to the music even more so. That is the reason it takes a talented, motivated student, attending class every day, approximately eight long years to master the craft—no small feat and one that merits high praise.

In the end, dancers must become a transparency for the music, whereby the music flows through their bodies and ultimately through their movements. Aural sensitivities are thus transformed into visual images. The question is whether these images accurately and truthfully illustrate the "collaborative" intent of the composer and the choreographer in a harmonious way. In the end, the revelation of the truth of that collaboration must become clearly evident. When done successfully, both the music and the dance are enhanced and true art is revealed.

CHAPTER 18 *Sprain or Strain?*

> The way to perfection is through
> a series of disgusts.
>
> Leonardo da Vinci

I wish to begin this brief chapter by disclaiming any professional medical expertise. I have no credentials, only many years of dancing and teaching experience. And I am also fortunate to have friends who are licensed physicians.

The stresses and physical challenges of exercises in ballet lessons are progressive. Each increasing physical demand is dependent on how well the preceding challenges have been assimilated. Being physically and mentally prepared for each new demand depends to a great extent on the work previously done.

Students who miss lessons or who habitually arrive late to class are neither physically nor mentally prepared for such demands, especially during the intermediate and advanced phases of study. Since the systematic warm-up that takes place in each lesson depends to a large extent on the work of previous exercises (classes), the body cannot be properly prepared to contend with the demands that follow if the continuum is broken. The risk of injury is greatly increased if this admonition is not followed, since the ballet lesson is scientifically designed to increase physical and mental demands. This is the way by which students safely contend with ever higher stresses and overcome the limitations of past efforts.

Lamentably, injuries are routine in most physical activities that push practitioners beyond the comfort zone. The most common injuries in ballet are sprains and strains. It is important to know the difference. Although teachers should not be performing the appropriate treatment for such injuries on their students, they need to know how to advise their students and parents and also how to follow up properly.

Sprains and strains result from overstretching or tearing soft tissues. The difference lies in where the injury is located. A sprain refers to an overstretched or torn ligament. A strain refers to an overstretched or torn muscle or tendon. Based on the severity, both can require anywhere from a few days to a few weeks of inactivity or reduced activity. More severe injuries may require surgery. However, I would always avoid surgery unless it proves to be the only remedy. If this is the recommended procedure, always get a second opinion from a specialist.

In either case, do not take such injuries lightly. It is usually best to consult an experienced sports medicine doctor to ensure the best and safest treatment. This applies even when you think the injury is minor.

Although there are other ways to treat injury, one should always follow the R.I.C.E. principle: Rest, Ice, Compression, and Elevation.

1. Rest the injury by not putting weight on the affected area for at least twenty-four hours.
2. Ice the area in intervals of twenty minutes (ice twenty minutes, no ice twenty minutes, repeat) to constrict injured blood vessels and also to decrease pain and swelling.
3. Compression using an elastic bandage or wrap can also reduce swelling.
4. Elevation (keeping the affected area raised above the level of the heart) helps to drain fluid from the injured area.

A sprain injury may be more serious than a strain and may therefore take more time to heal. Do not rush the healing process. Putting stress on the injured area prematurely can result in chronic problems. It is always a mistake to "work out the problem." And when resuming activity, go slowly and gently in the beginning. The purpose of recovering from an injury is to achieve a complete healing, not just relief. Our goal is to be able to resume normal activity without any recurrence of the problem.

Always remember the admonition to warm up before stretching. The two activities are not synonymous or interchangeable. Warming up is designed to induce and speed up blood flow, which produces heat in the affected area. On the other hand, a proper stretching regimen is designed to increase flexibility by elongating muscles, ligaments, and tendons that have already gone through a careful warming up process.

It is always a mistake to encourage or allow students to engage in radical stretching while they wait for the beginning of a lesson. Never stretch a cold body. This is only asking for trouble. It may feel good, but overstretched cold body parts tend to stiffen as they cool down. The misguided remedy for this is to stretch even more vigorously to overcome the stiffness. Always a mistake!

Taking medication to mask over chronic pain related to any of the above problems is equally inadvisable. No competent doctor would ever recommend such a procedure. Numbing the source of pain, by whatever method, only removes the symptom temporarily while allowing activity to exacerbate and possibly prolong the problem. Students and dancers should avoid such advice like the plague.

Like athletes, dancers need periods of rest when they do little intense activity. For example, ballet students in Russia take the entire summer off from their normal six-day week of intense work. It is felt that this period away from the rigors of the classroom is essential for the body to recuperate and also for the mind to relax from the stressful impositions of the daily grind. No doubt, some of these students begin to feel lazy during their break. Others may be itching to get back to the studio. Regardless, they will be resuming their regimen soon enough.

Unfortunately, this attitude is not the case in the United States. Here we send our students from course to course, intensive to intensive, master class to master class. Students feel the urgency to cram every possible experience into their schedules, and parents don't want them to miss a thing. But injury-free ballet studies are dependent on proper work, rest, and nutrition—a three-part formula that requires the blending of each element in order to reach optimum benefits.

Also, burnout is common with this hectic pace, which is absolutely unnecessary for young students to suffer through. Burnout can also lead to serious mental health problems, in addition to making the sufferer susceptible to physical injury and appetite and sleep disorders. Fatigue, both physical and mental, can have far-reaching effects.

Following an injury it takes nearly the same amount of time to return to peak condition as the time required for healing and recovery. Therefore, the return to health should follow a gradual resumption of exercises that avoids overstressing the affected area. There is no quick solution. Patience will have its reward.

Finally, no teacher, ballet master, choreographer, or company director should ever advise or encourage students or dancers to "work through" pain. Run for the nearest exit door if you hear such advice.

CHAPTER 19

Partnering Principles

> *For God's sake, give me the young man who*
> *has brains enough to make a fool of himself.*
>
> Robert Louis Stevenson

A discussion of partnering fundamentals evolves from an era of classical dance that is worth reviewing in order to gain insights. In the good old days of ballet history male dancers were generally relegated to the role of porteurs (carriers) of the ballerinas they partnered. They did not have much to do on their own as solo dancers. Many earned the title of "Premier Danseur" based exclusively on their skill at making the ballerina look good.

During the Romantic period of the early and mid-nineteenth century, ballet was considered a feminine art. Many themes of ballets created during that era emphasized the contrast between the sexes. This may have been due to the fact that classical dance had evolved from a previous era where there were virtually no female dancers at all. Male dancers even performed female roles "in drag," so to speak, much as the Kabuki theater actors in Japan still do today.

With few exceptions, this female-dominated dance situation lasted until the early twentieth century when Diaghilev's Ballets Russes took the world by storm. Extraordinary male dancers like the legendary Vaslav Nijinsky, Mikhail Mordkin, and Mikhail Fokine demonstrated that male dancers could hold their own against such famous female luminaries as Anna Pavlova, Olga Spessivtzeva, and Tamara Karsavina. By bringing such great male dancers to the West, the Ballets Russes exposed audiences to the possibilities of what male dancers could do on their own. These examples stimulated young men to take up the study of ballet in classes taught by retiring members of the Diaghilev Company who remained in the West following the Russian Revolution.

Meanwhile, in the new Soviet Union during the late 1910s and early 1920s, a new era of classical dance was being born. New ballets were choreographed that required male dancers to portray mighty heroes who fought and prevailed against evil. To accomplish this, they had to dance. The directors of the new Soviet art scene felt strongly that the days of sylphs and fairies had passed and that the Soviet public needed examples of strong male dancers capable of portraying the revolutionary spirit with balletic themes that demonstrated the triumph of the common man over oppression. It was widely felt that many of the old themes of classical ballet were too passive and trite.

During these precarious times, Agrippina Vaganova and a few other courageous souls assumed the onerous task of trying to convince revolutionary politicians that classical ballet deserved a place in the new Soviet society. It was an arduous uphill battle that very nearly cost the demise of classical ballet in Russia. We owe much to such dedicated visionaries who withstood the harshest criticisms to maintain what had heretofore been considered decadent entertainment reserved for the Imperial household and the upper classes.

During that trying period in 1925, Vaganova wrote in the magazine *Life in Art,* "Those who assert that the old ballet has spent itself and should be forgotten are deeply wrong. If art should, indeed, reflect contemporary life, it does not mean that classical examples of its past should disappear." She also wrote, "Give us a Soviet theme and then we shall succeed in producing a highly artistic Soviet production even with the idiom of old classical ballet. As to eccentric-acrobatic elements, they should occupy the modest one per cent that is their only worth."

Much of the success of this historic battle was due to having good teachers who taught and graduated several phenomenal male dancers who went on to set new standards that attracted much attention to this somewhat forgotten aspect of classical ballet. Dancers such as Asaf Messerer, Vakhtang Chabukiani, Pyotr Gusev, and Alexei Yermolayev were pioneers of this new era. They all had extraordinary technique that could dazzle audiences while they shared the limelight with the new generation of ballerinas whom they partnered.

The new repertoire excluded many of the ballets of the past. "Safe" themes that could pass the government censors were ballets that were either based on accepted literature by writers such as Pushkin, Gogol, Shakespeare, Hugo, and Balzac, or themes that emphasized the triumph of good over evil (the common man over the oppressor). Examples of new choreography of that period were *The Red Poppy, Fountain of Bakhchisarai, Flames of Paris, Esmeralda, Laurencia,* and *The Golden Age.* In addition, due to their enormous popularity, several masterpieces from the old repertoire survived, including *Swan Lake, Sleeping Beauty, Giselle, Raymonda, La Bayadère, Don Quixotè, Nutcracker,* and *Le Corsaire.*

While classical ballet struggled for survival in the Soviet Union, conditions around the world in other dancer "centers" remained much as before. There was only a handful of good teachers and very little sophistication in the populace to appreciate the demands of a good education in classical dance. Probably the most eminent ballet teacher of that era was Enrico Cecchetti, who did not return to Russia after leaving with Diaghilev's Ballets Russes.

Born in 1850, Cecchetti was nearly seventy years old when he retired from the stage to live and teach in England. After working with such legendary dancers as Anna Pavlova and Vaslav Nijinsky and many other great artists of the Ballets Russes, he was reduced to teaching daughters of wealthy society matrons and dance hall girls. Thus most of the western world still lagged behind Russia in the traditions of classical ballet education. It was not until initial contacts with the Bolshoi and Kirov touring companies in the late 1950s and early 1960s that things began to change.

So much for this brief history lesson. I have included it here to set the stage for the modern evolution of male dancing in the West that was impelled by the defection of Rudolf Nureyev in 1961 during a tour of the Kirov Ballet in Paris. It was one thing to see the many wonderful male dancers of the Russian touring companies perform. However, their KGB "minders" were never far away, and the dancers were protected from close scrutiny by curious western eyes. Now, with Nureyev in the West as a permanent member of the dance community, we were able to begin learning from his example. And he certainly piqued our interest.

There were also a handful of good male dancers working in the West during this period. Among them were Eric Bruhn, Igor Youskevitch, Andrei Eglevsky, and Anton Dolin. However, it was Nureyev's defection that showed us that male dancers could be much more than mere porteurs. They could stand on their own two feet and dazzle audiences just as effectively as the famous female dancers of the era. They only needed to be properly educated. But how to do this defied answers, at first. Then a few years later some intrepid teachers gained access to the "secrets" of the Vaganova method of instruction, which was the basis for Russian ballet training. At that time all Soviet ballet schools taught her system exclusively.

During that critical period there were a handful of ballet visionaries outside of Russia who perceived how important it was to learn why the Russians were so good. A few brave souls traveled to the Soviet Union and began knocking on doors. A handful were able to talk their way into the schools and convince administrators that they were serious about wanting to learn the "whys" and "hows." Little by little, once the message began to circulate, the flood tide became unstoppable. Vaganova's "secrets" were out.

Access to this invaluable information was greatly aided through translations from the original Russian language into English of textbooks on pedagogy. Until that time only Vaganova's own textbook was available. However, the information contained in her book was incomplete and only served to stimulate more questions. Armed with these new translations and personal experiences, serious teachers began to apply the newly discovered information.

One aspect of this discovery was related to partnering techniques. Until then, partnering was just an aspect of male dancing that was passed down from former dancers to their students. Nothing was codified or written into a curriculum. Therefore, the quality of partnering classes was entirely dependent on the knowledge of the teacher. Finally, the definitive book on teaching partnering technique was translated into English. *The Art of Pas de Deux,* written as a textbook for Russian teachers by Nikolai Serebrennikov in 1969, was translated into English by Joan Lawson in 1978. A subsequent translation by Elizabeth Kraft was published in 2000 by the University Press of Florida under the title *Pas de Deux: A Textbook on Partnering.* Until its publication, there was very little specific instruction available—mostly just the result of personal experiences of a few retired partners. However, it must be mentioned that Anton Dolin wrote a useful book on the subject entitled *Pas de Deux: The Art of Partnering*, published in New York in 1949. Although incomplete, it gave guidelines on how to work with a partner. Dolin was then a favorite partner of Alice Marks, an English girl who joined the Ballets Russes and was promptly renamed Alicia Markova by Serge Diaghilev, as was his custom with all non-Russian dancers who joined his company.

It is highly recommended that every teacher who teaches partnering techniques should own and use Serebrennikov's invaluable textbook. It contains both simple and complex exercises for students, who begin this specialized training at age fifteen or sixteen. Both students and teachers are taken step by step from the simplest fundamentals to the most intricate combinations. Great care is given to avoid even the remotest possibility of injury to either partner.

In Russia, students begin work on partnering during the final three years of their eight-year ballet course. At that time they are finishing their intermediate work and embarking on their final two years of learning advanced ballet technique. Until that point in their curriculum, they have not received specific classical partnering instruction. However, the boys and girls have already had some experience dancing together in folk dance, period dance, and character dance classes.

Starting specific classical pas de deux work before this age is unwise. The boys are not yet strong enough to lift and support the girls without the possibility of injury, and the girls are not yet strong enough on pointe to support themselves without overly relying on their partners to control balance and stability. It is essential that girls be able to support their own weight on pointe without any aid. And the boys should be close to the end of their final growth spurt, so that they do not lack the necessary strength of their backs and legs. Moderate weight training can also be beneficial.

It is both wise and logical, whenever possible, for partnering teachers to match boys and girls by height. The best proportion is when the girl is no taller than her partner when she is standing on pointe. Also, it is recommended that heavier girls be partnered by stronger boys. If partnering classes are to be given on a regular basis, it is wise to have the boys partner the same girls from class to class. This will help partnerships gel, as the two begin to get used to each other. Finally, if you have no other choice after the above considerations, put weaker girls together with stronger boys, and vice versa.

It must be determined that the girls are already strong in their own pointe work. They must be able to correctly execute all aspects of their own technique without assistance. If their legs or feet are wobbly, then they are not ready for partnering class. They should be able to do pirouettes alone, hold balances with strong backs, and rise onto their pointes without stress.

Next, it is essential that the girls realize that one of their partners' main functions is to help them do technical feats that are impossible for them to do alone. This means that the boys' main job is to help the girls turn more, balance longer, jump higher and farther, and control complex combinations—all done effortlessly and more beautifully than the girls can do on their own.

The boys' job is to make their partners look good at all times, even when it is uncomfortable or even precarious. In this respect, not much has changed during the past centuries. The boys are still essentially porteurs during the duet portions of pas de deux work.

One of the most important ideas to instill in the girls is that they must learn to completely trust their partners. They must never correct themselves. They must not try to fix balances that are falling, or leaning, or that feel awkward. Regardless of how uncomfortable they may feel, the girls must hold themselves according to the principles of the basic stance, *even when they are being held off balance by their partner*.

Sometimes it is obvious that it is the boy's fault when a pose or movement is off balance. Nevertheless, the girl must maintain her position until her partner fixes the problem. She must not move a muscle, or shift a single body part, or even subtly try to pull herself back to vertical alignment. Until her partner makes the necessary adjustments she is stuck. That is the nature of partnering. Of course, if her partner does not perform the necessary repairs, she might have a few words to say to him when the movement or combination is finished. However, if the girl makes any attempt at self-correction, her partner may have a few words to say to her—and rightly so.

It is important to understand that if the girl tries to remedy the situation on her own, she will only confuse the boy's attempts to find the correct equilibrium that will put her back on balance. In the beginning stages of learning partnering technique, this is often a huge problem for many girls because, heretofore, they have been working diligently to make every necessary adjustment to correct their own technical deficiencies or lapses. All of this acquired knowledge must be set aside, however. Now the girls are subject to their partners' understanding and sensitivity to their balance needs. Again, the girls must never attempt to self-correct. If their partner is holding them off balance, they must remain in that awkward position until the partner corrects the problem. Bite the bullet!

The boys need to develop sensitive hands, so that their partners' placement in all poses and positions feels weightless between their hands. Weight felt more in one hand than the other means that the girl is off balance. Take care of business!

Most of the time the boy's hands should rest firmly on top of the girl's hip bones. The thumb should be in back while the other four fingers are in front firmly holding the hip bone. The "wedge" of skin created between the thumb and the forefinger should apply firm (though not tight) inward pressure against the girl's waist just above the hip bone. Under no circumstances should the boy's hands be placed on or immediately below the rib cage. Pressure applied in this area causes much discomfort to the girl and may inhibit her breathing.

In his book, Serebrennikov differentiates between "feeling" and "holding" the girl. "Feeling" happens when the male partner is sensitive to the needs of the girl as she moves through the choreography. For example, the boy must understand what the girl needs when she moves from one pose or position to another, such as from or to an arabesque. In this particular pose, the girl's upper body moves forward and her pelvis tilts slightly as she positions her raised leg behind her. Later, the boy must be aware of the adjustments that must take place as the girl returns to vertical alignment or when she moves to a different ending position or pose.

There are other even more complex movements that require continuous adjustments, such as a grand rond de jambe, when the axis of vertical alignment is constantly changing as the working leg travels from the front around to the back, or vice versa. And there are innumerable mixed combinations of terre-à-terre movements, turns and lifts, all of which require different "feel" and "hold" contacts.

"Hold" contact is exemplified by all lifts. In addition, the boy must "hold" his girl at the end of a series of turns after "feeling" her balanced rotations.

There are a multitude of examples of "feeling" and "holding" that are carefully analyzed during the study of partnering. All of these movements demand the utmost consideration by the boys as they try to make their girls as comfortable as possible.

In addition to the admonition to not self-adjust, the girls must firmly hold themselves throughout every aspect of partnering. This is their proper role. Just as they learn to hold their positions when they dance alone, the girls must do the same when they are with a partner. However, holding themselves does not mean that they become unaware of other requirements of partnering. It must always appear to the viewer that the girls are performing while also being unobtrusively assisted by their partners. It must never appear that they are struggling to move in spite of someone hovering over them who is trying to correct awkward or out-of-balance poses.

When doing partnered pirouettes, the girl must do her own pirouettes. At the same time, her partner provides additional help for the required number of rotations and also for prolonging the balance. However, during turns that begin from a preparation while already standing on one leg, the girl must wait until she feels the turning impulse provided by her partner either on her waist or in her hands.

The boy's basic standing position should be a relaxed second position, with the heels about six to eight inches apart. This gives him a stable neutral stance that allows him the flexibility to move easily in any direction as dictated by the choreography and also the ability to adapt to the needs of his partner.

During partnering work, the boy must complement the girl's poses with poses of his own that add to the overall visual composition, according to the choreographer's wishes. Sometimes his pose might mirror the girl's arms and legs. Or his pose might be in opposition, which adds contrast and a more unique overall impression. In any case, the boy should never move too quickly to find his own pose. He must wait until he has helped the girl finish her movements. Or he may possibly make his move simultaneously with the girl, but only when he is certain that she is secure.

Both partners also need to develop certain intangibles involving rhythm and tempo. They must learn to feel and react to each other's movements so their combined movements are precisely coordinated with each other. In this regard there is more of an onus on the male half of the partnership to make sure that he assists and guides his partner through the movements she is executing. Partnering instructors need to be aware of this important detail. Attention to this aspect of partnering will lead to a beautifully harmonious blending of artistic qualities.

It must appear to viewers that the partners are "communicating" with each other. There should be no lapse of timing as the two move through their dancing phrases together. It should seem as though they are dancing as one. Nothing should appear forced as they are guided through the choreography by the music. Neither the boy nor the girl should feel that they are struggling with each other's timing to stay with the music. Even their breathing should be coordinated, breathing through their noses, so that their faces are relaxed and free to address the requirements of expression in the portrayal of their roles.

Partnering is an art. Good partnerships are rare and memorable when they happen. It is common today for top-level ballerinas and male dancers to guest with various companies over the course of a year. When dancers travel from company to company, it is impossible to establish a relationship with a regular partner, unless they travel as a pair. Therefore, individual dancers in this category must be very strong, since they may be required to dance with many partners. This is not a desirable situation, as each partner must then become accustomed to a new partner's idiosyncrasies. The female may need to be more aggressive with one partner and less with another. The male may only need to help guide his partner through her movements with one ballerina, while providing stronger "feel" and "hold" techniques with another. The ability to adapt has become an important aspect of the partnering art.

Since the classical pas de deux danced by principal artists is a highlight of many classical ballets, it is natural that each participant would want to excel in his or her part. The paradox is that neither partner wants to be outdone by the other, while each wants to perform with an accomplished artist who will contribute to the whole performance. Just the right balance is sought after. In today's hurry-scurry of minimal rehearsals, travel requirements, and performance preparations, it is difficult to find the right formula that satisfies everyone.

It is not so common today to hear about great partnerships such as we enjoyed in the past: Alicia Alonso and Igor Youskevitch, Alicia Markova and Anton Dolin, and Margot Fonteyn and Rudolf Nureyev dancing in the

West. In Russia we saw or heard about such partnerships as Galina Ulanova and Nicolai Fadeyechev, Ekaterina Maximova and Vladimir Vasiliev, and Natalia Dudinskaya and Konstantin Sergeyev. All of these partnerships brought the art of classical dance to new heights. They transcended the mere accompaniment of dancers with each other. Their individual artistic input was compounded into a partnership that approached the sublime.

How were these great partnerships accomplished? First of all, these artists danced together repeatedly, and by doing so they became familiar with each other's needs. The choreography of steps got lost in the art that each one brought to the team. While their movements were seamlessly smooth, their emotions were genuinely felt and transmitted to the audience, leaving an indelible impression.

Naturally, students in partnering classes are not expected to arrive at such artistic heights. However, by adhering to important guidelines and learning how to immerse themselves into the partnership, the first steps are taken. After learning the fundamentals, novice partners begin to understand how each one's contribution to the partnership adds to the entire visual and sensual impression. They will begin to feel a harmonious relationship while also dancing smoothly together.

In today's world of eclectic choreography, it would be impossible for a ballerina to dance exclusively with the same partner night after night. It would also be far too exhausting. Indeed, of the aforementioned ballet partnerships, all of the participants danced from time to time with others. The requirements of the choreography and appropriateness of characterization often determine such factors.

It has been said that good male partners are born. It is clear that they all possess the same instinct and love of this aspect of classical dancing. Most classical pas de deux express the epitome of gentlemanly art. The role of the male is often that of a selfless cavalier. His job is to make his ballerina look her best, even when it means that he must sacrifice himself to do so. His is an unselfish role, even when he knows that a taxing and demanding variation awaits him only a few minutes later. Male partners who embody this demand of classical dance are always appreciated by their female counterparts and their audiences.

In advanced partnering classes, a practice tutu can be used by the girl. But it is best in elementary classes for the girl to dress in plain leotard and tights. Since both the boy and the girl are learning this new technique, nothing should interfere with the requirements of "hold" and "feel." The girl's waistline should be smooth and uncluttered by skirts, warmers, etc. The girl should wear broken-in pointe shoes, neither too soft nor too hard.

In Serebrennikov's book it can be seen that elementary partnering exercises are very simple. In the beginning, the girls must learn to trust their partners implicitly. They must also learn to allow their partners to correct balance problems and not self-correct. These important details can only be accomplished through a slow, methodical process.

For example, a good beginning exercise is for the teacher to have the girl relevé onto pointe in fifth position with her arms held in first position while the boy holds her by the waist. The boy should try to find the point of weightlessness between his hands, not too far forward, backward, or sideways (left-right). Once both partners are comfortable with this simple exercise, it can be repeated by having the boy purposely move the girl slightly off balance, either forward, backward, or sideways, and then return to the "weightless" center balanced position before the girl comes down from pointe.

Once this simple exercise is correctly done, it can be repeated using other simple positions while standing on one leg such as retiré front and back, and with the arms held in different positions. Finally, the same exercise can be done in all poses and positions. This approach teaches both partners to work together and trust each other. It lays the foundation for a solid partnership in the future while instilling confidence in both partners.

Even though boys and girls learn to correctly employ good partnering principles, each partner is different. The boy must learn to adapt to the idiosyncrasies of each girl he works with, and vice versa. Although the same fundamentals apply to all equally, there are always subtle differences from one dancer to another. A good male partner must become sensitive to the differences.

There are many reasons for this. Some dancers are shorter or taller; some are more turned-out than others; some are more flexible than others; each feels her center of vertical alignment differently; hyperextension affects balance; and some girls need to feel more assisted as they move, while others want their partners to give them space. This means that each participant must be flexible . Good male partners make the transition smoothly, so that new female partners feel no discomfort while adjustments are being made.

Each ballerina must be partnered differently. This is normal. And it is incumbent on the male to do his utmost so that his partner feels comfortable at all times. This is especially important when the girl transfers her weight from one step (or pose) to another. She should not have to struggle to make adjustments by twisting or leaning while being held by her partner. Such timing problems or imbalances spoil the effortless impression that a smooth partnership should impart. It is helpful if the girl is able to get herself into position and hold it until she and her partner have finished the required movement. Then she and her partner can move on to whatever follows in a coordinated manner. Timing mishaps can be avoided if this rule is followed.

The characterization, music, and choreography also determine how ballerinas should be partnered. Different ballets require different approaches. Some ballets require a more reverent approach, while others demand a stronger, more resolute approach. For example, there should be a clear difference between performing the pas de deux from *Don Quixote* and from *Giselle*. And there is an even more striking difference between the pas de deux from *Sleeping Beauty* and from *Les Sylphides*. Each role has its own identity and requires a different approach to partnering demands.

Finally, a great partnership is a collaboration. There are elements of individual exhibitionism, to be sure, but neither partner should focus on rising above at the other's expense. There should never be a display or hint of one-upmanship. The best male partner is one who appears self-effacing. His job is to show off his ballerina to the audience in the best possible light. However, when it is his turn to dance alone, he then has an opportunity to give the audience something to remember. He is not a mere porteur any longer.

The best female partner is not quite so self-effacing. She generally takes her position in front of her partner, who helps her spin more pirouettes than she can do alone. He also helps her balance and sustain poses. And he lifts her into prolonged soaring leaps and tosses that she could never perform without his assistance. Most of these basic partnering techniques are done while the boy stands behind the girl, and they must always be done artistically without showing any sign of effort.

The real beauty of the ideal classical ballet partnership rests in the completeness of a harmonious whole that transcends individual talents. It is an aspect of the art of classical dance that demands careful study.

CHAPTER 20 *Introduction to Pantomime for Dancers*

Gesture is the second organ of speech, which
nature has given to man, but it can be heard
only when the soul orders it to speak.

Jean Georges Noverre

The theater is an imitation of life. As such, it changes as time goes on. Actors should not copy the acting style or skills of others. The same applies to dancers, who should find their own style, expressing themselves naturally and simply.

When dancing a role, the primary aim as dancer/actor is to fascinate audiences by an interpretation of the choreography and emotions associated with it. To accomplish this, dancers must learn how to stimulate their powers of imagination, so that they can call on their emotions at will at any time as needed by the character they are playing. Certain exercises and practice can help them develop this ability.

In the following pages, I will give some sample lessons designed to introduce important aspects of acting as they relate to dancing. These exercises are based on Konstantin Stanislavski's acting methodology. Stanislavski was the founder of the Moscow Arts Theater in the late nineteenth century. His system provided the foundation of the so-called method style used widely in American acting schools since the early 1950s.

In the early days of the Russian Revolution, Alexander Gorsky, successor to Marius Petipa as principal choreographer-director of the Ballet Company, was especially interested in Stanislavski's ideas. Eventually, Stanislavski-trained acting teachers gave pantomime/acting classes in the state ballet schools as part of their regular curriculum. The goal was to work toward the development of a natural expression, while eliminating mannerisms and clichés.

The purpose is to create a living, truthful object on the stage, whether it is a human being or a fanciful creature, or even if it is simply an emotion for its own sake (such as Balanchine's *Four Temperaments*). To accomplish this in a believable way, the actor must be inwardly convinced that he exists through his character—and not just pretend to exist. A true actor sees himself in his character, not the character in him. He becomes the character.

We have often heard of the importance of "inspiration" on the stage. But inspiration is an accidental thing. We must work conscientiously to acquire the ability to focus attention on the intended goal and not wait for inspiration. This is just as important in the classroom and rehearsal studio as it is onstage. What happens if you wait for inspiration and it does not come? Who is to blame?

Without great choreographers there would be no art of ballet. Therefore, it is the dancer's first duty to faithfully create the character that the choreographer conceives, as well as follow the patterns of movement that he designs as accurately as possible. For this reason rehearsals must be taken very seriously. The truly dedicated artist will use every rehearsal to give the choreographer exactly what he requires, while constantly searching for ways to improve his own artistic interpretation.

The conscientious artist also realizes that he must carefully watch others; learn from their mistakes and his own; resist the temptation to be depressed or discouraged; listen attentively; and assimilate direction and corrections. In other words, he must use every class and rehearsal as an opportunity to learn. Anything less is self-imposed limitation. Professional dancers must not wait for or expect inspiration from those they are working with. It must come from within. This is being a professional artist! The same applies to students beginning to learn the art.

The art of ballet is based on collective work. It is essential that everyone in the group work for the benefit of the whole performance and not only for himself. Such discipline is indispensable. Dancing before the public is not only a challenge but also a privilege and a responsibility to the audience. Remember, they are paying to see a finished artistic product, not a work in progress that may or may not ever get polished. A real dancer respects his profession so that the audience can learn to love and respect the art of ballet.

It is important to remember the following:

1. Acting, both vocal and pantomimed, is a way of expressing truth in a personal way through the creation of a character or emotion.
2. It is imperative to penetrate the spirit of the character you are portraying. This includes the inner motivation of the movement itself.
3. Love the art in yourself rather than yourself in the art. Egoism is a crippling limitation in a true artist.
4. The theater infects the audience with its noble ecstasy.
5. There are no small parts, only small actors.
6. The difficult must become a habit; habit must become easy and the easy beautiful.
7. Always create consciously and truthfully.
8. The key to successful pantomime is achieving superrealism (more real than life itself).
9. The art of the theater is based on a uniting of the deep substance of the inner life and a beautifully expressive demonstration of it.
10. Work for simplicity.
11. Details, details, details! They are what make the artistic gift package complete.
12. Focus on the joy of expressing your art, not on how difficult it is.
13. Turn off the voice in your head that tries to convince you that you can't do something. You must believe that all things are possible.
14. The pathway to artistic heights is an arduous climb. Learn to enjoy the process, even while the journey is difficult.

Because of stage fright, nerves, and the demands of accurately dancing predetermined choreography in front of an audience, we tend to lose the feeling of real life. Normal human sensations become elusive. We tend to forget how to do the simplest things naturally, and normal day-to-day movements become stilted and awkward.

The following exercises will help dancers return to their natural selves on stage:

PANTOMIME LESSON 1: *Justification*

On the stage there must always be an inner action, an outer action, or both. These actions comprise everything the actor does on the stage, including all movements and expressions of emotion. And they must be justified. In other words, they must have a purpose and be logical. Otherwise they will not be convincing to the viewer. There must also be an inner motivation for every action, and the actor must do it for his own reasons, not merely because it is in the script or because the choreographer says so. In other words, he must do it as if he were doing it in real life.

Exercise: Do the following actions as if something in your real life demands it. Justify what you are doing.

1. While you are standing—stretch one leg forward and spread your arms open in any way you like.
2. While you are standing—stretch one arm high overhead and look down at the floor. Use your other arm in any way you like.
3. Two people are seated at a table. One stands up, walks three steps away from the table, stops, and then turns back toward the second person, who is seated and observing him. He then places both hands on his forehead. The second person remains seated watching until the first turns and touches his forehead. The second then stands up and points at him.

Exercise: Do a convincing portrayal of the following inanimate objects (no vocals, and remain in one place).

1. Telephone
2. Refrigerator
3. Television set
4. Record player
5. Sewing machine
6. Flash camera
7. Steam iron
8. Vending machine
9. Mousetrap
10. Typewriter

PANTOMIME LESSON 2: *Imagination*

The job of an actor is to transform the story into an artistic reality. To do this, the actor's imagination must be developed. He must be able to direct his concentration; notice what is around him; be able to dream; and, more important, be able to participate in his dreams so they become real. When given a dramatic role, the actor must complete the character by filling in any gaps left by the creator, whether a playwright or a choreographer. This is how he will give substance to the character. Everything he imagines must be precise and logical, otherwise it won't be convincing to the audience.

Exercise: Show a photograph of a person.

1. Who is he?
2. What is his profession?
3. Where does he live?
4. Is he married?
5. Does he have children? How many? What are their names? How old are they?
6. What kind of home does he live in? Describe it in detail.
7. What is his personality like?
8. What are his tastes?
9. Does he have a hobby?
10. What kind of car does he drive?
11. What is his favorite food?
12. What kind of music does he like?
13. What is his favorite movie?

Exercise: I want to get to know you better, so I'm going to ask you some questions. Assume that the facts are correct. Do your best to engage me in your answers so that I become interested in what you are saying. You are hoping that I will like you and ask you out for another date.

1. Did you enjoy last night's party?
2. Who was that you were speaking with on the phone just now when I arrived? What did he say?
3. Where do you plan to go on your vacation?
4. Why did you choose that place for your vacation?
5. Why do you suppose that you are afraid of flying?

6. Would you like me to help you with your homework project?

7. Would you like to go to a movie with me next Saturday? And maybe grab a hamburger afterward?

Exercise: Take a trip around the world. Describe it to a friend. Be consecutive, logical, and detailed.

Exercise: Finish the following phrases logically.

1. "I enjoyed my blind date, but . . .
2. "I was late to school this morning, and my teacher . . .
3. "My mother said that I couldn't go, because . . .
4. "I went shopping for a new formal dress, and . . .
5. "We decided to accept the invitation, since . . .
6. "My father took my cell phone away, because . . .

Exercise: Do a convincing portrayal of the following animals (no vocals, but you can move around a little).

1. Peacock
2. Mouse
3. Woodpecker
4. Siamese cat
5. Rabbit
6. King cobra
7. Giraffe
8. Turtle
9. Mosquito
10. Thoroughbred racehorse

Exercise: "The Mirror"

The "mirror" exercise involves two people. One is the "subject," and the other is the "mirror." The subject stands in front of the mirror primping, combing, applying makeup, scratching, rubbing, making faces, etc. The mirror copies everything the subject does, to the smallest detail.

Other exercises further refine concentration abilities. Some are based on the sense of hearing:

1. A reader tries to convince listeners of an important message. However, he must do so while being heckled by one of the listeners.
2. A heckler distracts someone trying to solve a math problem or memorize a short poem.

Another hearing exercise can be done by having students sit outside or open the windows and doors for a few minutes, and then compile a list of the different sounds that they hear. Other hearing exercises could include:

1. Whisper a story to someone, which he/she will repeat to someone else. Compare the final story with the original.
2. You are studying quietly in your room when someone you can't stand calls you on the phone.
3. The doorbell rings. Your dog begins barking and won't stop. Your friend outside is afraid of the dog.
4. It is a stormy night, and you are alone. Suddenly you hear a noise downstairs.

Other exercises that expand the imagination are as follows:

1. You take a seat in a movie theater. Later, someone very tall sits directly in front of you. There is no other seat to move to.
2. You are waiting at a bus stop. The bus is late, and you are in a hurry.
3. You sit down to rest in a park after a long day of shopping. You have several packages. It begins to rain.
4. You are standing in a crowd trying to watch a parade.
5. You are standing in a long line waiting to buy tickets for a performance you are dying to see. They will be sold out soon.
6. You are walking quickly to class when you see someone you like approaching. The bell rings, and you can't be late.
7. You are walking back and forth across the room in order to annoy the neighbor below, who has been nasty to you recently.

Other more complex exercises might be:

1. You are the teacher of a ballet class of small children. You take attendance by asking each student his or her name. Then someone comes in late. When you double-check your roll by taking a head count, you find that you have missed someone.

2. You and a friend went to an audition. You are both standing in line while the choreographer calls the names of those he has chosen. He picks your friend but not you. Everyone is then dismissed. As you are going out the door with your friend, you are called back by the choreographer and told that he had mislaid your name and that you were chosen after all.

The next exercise involves natural phenomena. Do a convincing portrayal of the following (no sounds):

1. Blazing fire
2. Stormy water
3. Summer breezes
4. Hot sun
5. Rain (sprinkle, shower, downpour)
6. Placid water
7. Fog
8. Plant growing
9. Volcano

There are many other invaluable exercises. However, most entail more involved speaking assignments and are therefore somewhat less important for future dancers, who are more interested in learning pantomime skills.

Only an audience with dazzled eyes grieves when, onstage,
a skillful actor dies. The curtain falls. The fallen actor rises.

Anonymous

CHAPTER 21 *Which Is More Important, Learning or Self-Esteem?*

*One does nothing good without passion,
nothing excellent by passion alone.*

Nadia Boulanger

The task of pedagogy is to transfer knowledge to receptive minds, so that recipients eagerly and joyfully pursue the possibilities of even greater understanding. The field of education, in all areas, is struggling with how to engage and maintain students' interest. This is true in academia as well as in the arts. But which is most important in the education process, learning or self-esteem?

There are two schools of thought. Some educators take the view that, unless learning is fun, students will become bored and tune out. They believe that rewards and praise are necessary to further stimulate work. The other school of thought believes that competency is gained through practice and perseverance. Each side is convinced that they are correct in their approach, but they freely admit that the other has some merit. The more modern approach is the former "feel good" method. The more traditional approach is the latter, which emphasizes that excellence can only be achieved through discipline and work.

In studying piano, it is more fun to learn sonatas and études than to practice scales and fingering exercises. Likewise, in dance, it is more fun to perform in recitals and competitions than to perfect fundamentals in the classroom. And athletes would much rather play a game than spend time in the gym or on the field practicing technical drills.

Critics of the "feel good" approach insist that pursuing the ever elusive goal of excellence must be a priority. They say that, while it is important to engage students in the fun of learning, the minimums of practice inherent in emphasizing the performance aspect of the activity are not sufficient to develop outstanding executants. They decry the tendency toward boundless praise and rewarding minimal effort. And even worse, they criticize tolerating mediocrity to bolster self-esteem.

On the other hand, advocates of the self-esteem approach criticize the focused-learning method. They claim that rote repetitiveness stifles enjoyment of the pursuit and that drill becomes tedious. They admit that practice is necessary, but they insist that the required work is inherent in the game or the performance of the activity.

There is truth in both concepts. However, in the case of classical ballet, teachers must constantly remind themselves that nearly everything their students do is new and challenging for them when first explained, whether it is a physical or a mental test. We sometimes forget how it felt when we were students ourselves. We forget how difficult it was to master new challenges and new ideas and how great it felt when we finally figured it out.

Self-esteem is important in developing superior skills and utilizing talents. Under the tutelage of a true pedagogue, students learn that focused hard work pays off. Therefore, self-esteem may be a by-product of the "hard work" method of learning. This is a process of self-discovery, which is the most rewarding source of feeling good about oneself. A high goal attained or a difficulty mastered is very satisfying. But praise for minimal effort and mediocre performance is rather empty, because it gives the recipient the wrong message. It says that a B– or a C+ grade is good enough and that additional effort is unnecessary because one must focus on new challenges that need to be confronted.

Competitive ice skaters in the Olympic Games are expected to perform certain skating patterns to demonstrate technical precision even while engaged in free-style segments of the competition. If they do not perform certain technical skills to perfection, they will not win high scores. This is also true in gymnastics, diving, and other events. It is apparent that participants in these activities derive their technical superiority through focused hard work. Also, the beautiful and elegant way that skaters perform their skills is an additional layer of artistry that transcends mere technical achievement.

Why is it not the same with other physical and intellectual pursuits? Is it because hard work is not considered fun?

Enjoyment is not ultimately achieved through diversion and constantly trying out new things but through the progression of successful efforts, whether it is learning a new sport, beginning a new job, or engaging in an artistic pursuit. Keep in mind that an effort analogous to a shotgun blast may obliterate the target, but a single bull's-eye shot that zeroes in on a specific goal is more precise and satisfying. Trying out many new things is fun at first, but students eventually become frustrated when they discover that they cannot execute or perform new challenges the way they are supposed to be done.

Playing a Mozart sonata without any "clinkers" is very satisfying. Dancing an impeccable "Sugar Plum Variation" without a single faux pas is a thrill. And hitting a grand-slam home run to win a championship baseball game is truly memorable. Not all students will achieve such measures of success. This is to be expected. But unless they try their hardest, encouraged and coaxed on by their teachers, excellence will always remain unattainable. Excellence is the realm where self-esteem is to be found. Feeling good about a mediocre effort is faint reward and merits little praise.

Both educational approaches—focused, disciplined hard work and fun-seeking self-esteem—should be given importance. Both are indispensable and cannot exist without the other. However, if I had to make a choice of one over the other, I would lean toward the hard work approach. It is a method that has demonstrated an extraordinary record of achievement in all areas of human endeavor, with satisfying long-term rewards.

CHAPTER 22

Geido *(Artistic Ways)*

Art is long and life is brief.

Senaca

Geido means "artistic ways" in the Japanese language. Although *geido* is used to describe an aspect of martial arts, it is pertinent in a discussion of self-enrichment or finding oneself through the arts—a way to personally experience an art form.

Geido involves actions that create or re-create cultural values through physical means, while demanding a complete mental and spiritual commitment. The actions of *geido* also result in a cultural product. However, the product is subservient to the process of creating it. The value for the engaged individual, therefore, lies in the doing—the process rather than in the results. This means that students are required to strive to develop abilities and techniques to perfection, in other words, mastery.

Undoubtedly, to achieve mastery, it is crucial to select a good teacher. Then, through studied practice, the student arrives at a state of self-discovery, a clear understanding of the principles of his or her art, through experiences, not just instruction. Technical mastery of the *do* (way) is the realization that mastery is not exclusively an intellectual process. It must be experienced.

One learns how to dance by means of educating the body. The body is the entity that houses the intangibles of the mind and spirit. Training the body does not differentiate between physical drills and mental understanding. To achieve results there must be a unified mind-body approach. Their functions are inseparable. It is oneness (receptiveness) of these two interdependent halves of training that allows the body to master technique. However, the skillful execution of movement without acute mental involvement (artistry) is just dry and mindless. It may momentarily excite the viewer but leaves no lasting impression. Therefore, artistry demands the unification of both mind and body.

It is more difficult to train the mental side of the equation, because the mind does not always remain focused on the task at hand. It sometimes drifts. And when it does, accurate analysis is virtually impossible. It is even possible for the body to respond more or less correctly during such lapses due to reinforced habit. However, the result is usually not very satisfying. It is imperative that students mentally zero in on their physical assignments without any outside distractions. This requires a refined level of conscientiousness that is not very common with most young neophytes and needs to be learned—a daunting challenge that faces all teachers.

The mental side of practice is always in a state of flux. The mind should never fixate on a single idea, no matter how important. Otherwise, dance cannot become art. It will just be a series of disjointed and meaningless movements—possibly well executed, but nevertheless a boring exhibition of steps. Viewers of a dancer (whether onstage or in the studio) should never be distracted by the artist's technique. Technique must be subservient to and subject to the art. It is only a facilitating tool.

However, a mind that focuses too acutely fixates on the objects of thought. This prevents the fluidity of the art from flowing through the body and stultifies expressiveness in the face and eyes. The mind must not focus on a single thought. When artists just let their art flow through, they discover that there is no need to focus on a specific idea or physical challenge. In the case of dance, the flow will then become spontaneous and natural, although elevated to superhuman levels through technical refinement. The mind that flows through the body without fixating on any specific thing is a "free" mind, thus attaining *geido*.

In the martial arts, achieving this level of "mindlessness" is one of the ultimate goals. While engaged in a mock-combat situation, the controlled "mindless" participant just frees his active mind and responds automatically to the stimulus (attack or defense). There is no plan for proposed actions. There is no celebration or regret for any action taken. And there must never be any midstream analysis of actions previously taken, especially as they pertain to mistakes that may occur. Most participants never achieve this state of mental discipline and thus fall short of true achievement. That is why achieving excellence is so difficult.

An important aspect of perfecting technique is the concept of learning from past mistakes (or successes). In this regard, rote repetition is appropriate in the beginning of the training process. At elementary levels, training should be kept simple to avoid mental resistance. Premature embellishments distract the nascent mind and cause it to focus too intently on the complex new challenges. Constant polishing and refining leads to the desired goal of establishing good habits and the eventual complete understanding of every detail and nuance—in other words, mastery. When this level has been achieved, unique individual qualities may be injected without interrupting the flow of artistic expression.

In the early stages of training, it is important to preserve the precision of technical development. Later, the accomplished artist can successfully liberate himself from the demands of technical precision so that true creative individuality can be expressed. However, due to its complexity, elementary training must be rigorous and demanding, requiring no less than the utmost physical and mental concentration from the student.

To achieve the highest levels of artistry, one must be somewhat cut off from the mundane world. Perfecting an art such as classical ballet demands that one must concentrate obediently on the pure process of learning its subtle nuances. There is little in a young hopeful's life that approximates the pursuit of such a high goal. Therefore, one must focus single-mindedly on this process and not just during the hours spent in the classroom.

Ironically, such a level of commitment influences behavior and carries over into life and the ability to adapt to many of life's challenges. This ability is one of the definitions of "intelligence." In classical ballet at its highest expression, intelligence is imperative to the attainment of excellence. Therefore, one must exercise the mind as well as the body.

CHAPTER 23 *Choreography's Role in Classical Ballet*

Life rushes from within, not from without. There is no work of art so big or so beautiful that it was not once all contained in some youthful body.

Willa Cather

It is on choreographers' shoulders that the future of classical ballet falls. This onus has always been the case, at least for the last two centuries of ballet's existence. During most of the nineteenth and first half of the twentieth centuries, great ballet creators rose to the challenge. Enduring classics danced by some of the greatest artists in ballet history established this period as the golden age of classical dance. However, for nearly fifty years there has been a paucity of great choreographers. This is a continuing problem that tempts ballet lovers and skeptics alike to declare that classical ballet may be passé. But can this be true?

Where are the great new choreographers? Are any contemporary choreographers capable of creating major classical works that will live on their own merits beyond the creators' lifetimes? Where are the new Petipas, the Fokines, the Tudors, the new Ashtons, Crankos, and MacMillans, and the Grigorovichs? Where are the Balanchines?

I can already hear the grumbling of outraged protestations concerning the above assertion. Yes, indeed, there are people working today who are attracting attention and a certain amount of critical acclaim, even high praise from some sources. However, let's be honest. Do any of their efforts rise to the artistic heights of a *Swan Lake,* a *Coppelia,* or a *Sleeping Beauty*?

It would seem that choreographers today are more interested in abstract contemporary works and revamping time-tested ballets than risking the creation of new major works. For example, more than a dozen versions of *Romeo and Juliet* have been created since the 1940 world premiere of Prokofiev's direct collaboration with choreographer Leonid Lavrovsky. But isn't it somewhat egoistic to believe that one can improve on a masterwork? Nevertheless, it seems that we are suffering an era of revisionism.

I hasten to add that some interesting contemporary works are being done. However, most are short pieces that are used by company directors to help fill typical three-bill programs. But will any of these new works live beyond the lives of their creators? Only time will tell. Meanwhile, classical ballet is plodding through an era of the doldrums.

The great tragedy in the theater is that the attempt to create art is only that—an attempt. Creators hope that their efforts are justified by an appreciative audience. Otherwise, their works will certainly die. Most often a work dies because it deserves to and will justifiably be forgotten. To be considered true art, the work must be meaningful. It must touch audiences and leave a lasting impression. True art creates its own life and is reborn in the minds of the audience each time it is performed. If it is unable to do this, it is merely a clever or pretty thing that has its moment but is soon forgotten.

Before anything else, artists are skilled craftsmen. And what is always fundamental is that artists, when creating good art, employ their skills and imagination in exceptional ways. It is conceivable that a choreographer might create something wonderful. But if the dancers he employs are unskilled; or the music he chooses is hard on the ears; or the costumes, lighting, or scenery are inappropriate; then the work is doomed. The intrinsic value of a choreographic work lies in how successfully all of the intended images are revealed. The dancers must also actively contribute to this revelation and not just perform steps, no matter how well executed they may be.

The challenge in celebrating good dance is to create choreography that provides dance artists an opportunity to use well-harmonized physical movements convincingly to express inner emotions that are meaningful to viewers. In this regard choreographers and dancers need each other. The finished product is only as strong as the weakest link. Therefore, to create real art, all contributors must be highly proficient, and there must be mutual trust. The problem arises when choreographers create for themselves as a personal artistic outlet and not for their audiences.

The indispensable collaboration between the artists—choreographer, dancers, and musicians—must be refined so that the work speaks with clarity to the audience. It has to be able to reach them, to enrich, to excite, and, yes, even to entertain them. Choreography potentially speaks a universal language that is capable of uniting peoples and cultures. Good choreography accomplishes this goal. It is the common thread that links the past with the present and indicates the future.

It is incumbent on each ballet organization to clearly outline its mission and establish plans for achieving its goals. And this must be realistically done. Meanwhile, far too many well-intentioned community and civic ballet organizations are presenting abbreviated and/or revised versions of the classics danced by companies too small to properly present full-length productions. Such companies need to reevaluate their purpose, remembering that an important aspect of theater is education, in addition to entertainment.

The illusions presented on stage may be fantasy or realistic, comedic or dramatic, or they may just be well-designed danced interpretations of good music. Regardless, viewers must be allowed to penetrate the artistic experience and be elevated to a level unattainable in any other context. To achieve this higher purpose, the theater cannot simply become a commercial enterprise used to pay a choreographer's fee or dancers' salaries. High ticket prices that are only affordable to patrons and balletomanes turn less affluent audiences away.

Another important issue needs to be addressed. Paradoxically, the golden age of ballet was dominated by male creators, even though thematic emphasis usually featured the ballerina as the primary attraction, with the male dancer's role mainly as that of porteur. The scarcity of master choreographers today seems to have opened the door to choreographic opportunities for women. But in spite of greater opportunities, women continue to suffer from a male-dominated art specialization. Witness how few women are notable classical music composers, architects, painters, and sculptors. Although they have made notable strides in other fields such as literature, chauvinism is still evident in many of the arts.

I do not believe that women are incapable creators or that they lack sufficient imagination to create masterworks. Nevertheless, history reveals that on select lists of most artistic fields, there appear more men than women. There is also a mistaken perception by male artists that women lack authority in their fields and that they struggle unduly to obtain optimum cooperation from their male participants. It seems to be difficult for men to concede high levels of creative recognition to women, even when talent is clearly evident. Let's hope that this lamentable condition does not continue.

In the early days, choreographers studied sculpture as a means of penetrating the essence of plasticity even within a static object. Great sculptural masterworks seem to breathe, to express living feelings, even though they may consist of bronze or marble. It is said that the sculptor's job is to remove all that is superfluous from the block of raw material that he begins to work with. His job is also to find order in the chaos of movement and expressive possibilities.

Choreographers have a similar responsibility. Their job is to elevate earthly order to a much higher level than is apparent to most viewers. In doing so, their work has to transcend mere decoration and superficial prettiness. However, the order they create has to rise above idiosyncratic mannerisms and insider messages. And most important, the order that choreographers create must never reflect egomania. What they do is for others. It must be selfless, not self-indulgent.

It is not enough to be voguish or caught up in the styles of the moment. Also, choreographers' work must not be predictable or prosaic. The order that they create must make the story, emotions, and characters come to life in ways that audiences can relate to and learn from.

The choreographer's primary task is to communicate, and to accomplish this, a choreographer needs at least one other person with whom to share his insights. The shared artistic product is a form of communication. It may be an original concept, or it may just be a new way of communicating old ideas, such as emotions, that we all can understand.

What the choreographer does is coordinate communication so that the ideas flow effortlessly between the performers and audiences. This implies that some kind of exchange takes place between the creators and viewers. Therefore, choreographic art needs an audience. But what does the choreographer receive from the audience to complete the circuit? An acknowledgment that he has successfully related his intentions in telling the story or elevating the viewer to another level of insight.

If one analyzes many of the great balletic masterpieces, their story lines are uncomplicated, sometimes even simplistic. Good triumphing over evil and love overcoming all obstacles are popular themes. The good guy wears a white hat, and the bad guy a black one. The ballerina is beautiful, and the prince is handsome.

Some contemporary critics might say that all this is trite and silly. However, it has been established that audiences deeply feel an urge to experience such clearly defined roles. After all, they are the values that most of us aspire to in our daily lives. We want to be able to identify good and evil so that we can make decisions that will guide our lives. And we all thrive on loving relationships. This is our hope when we watch a play, an opera, or a ballet classic.

Viewers are not particularly interested in watching protagonists struggle and fail, even though we are all aware that it happens in life. Most of us aspire to better times. Tomorrow will be a better day. Somewhere over the rainbow. Therefore, it is appropriate for art creators to understand what audiences hunger for. It goes without saying that art can be poignant, even critical, when it attempts to point out human foibles and errors. But a steady diet of "heavy" art eventually becomes disheartening. And one yearns for solutions, not just commiseration. No one enjoys leaving a performance depressed. The theater should be a place where messages are uplifting, where there is hope, where realities are revealed and solutions are proposed.

The audience should never leave the theater wondering about the intent of the choreographer. The message should be clear, even when the creation is nothing more than pure movement. If choreographers only create for connoisseurs and critics with refined sensibilities, they will be missing the point of their calling. If the primary purpose of art is communication, then insider "conversations" are inappropriate. We are not trying to conceal coded messages that can only be deciphered by experts. The work must connect with the widest possible audience to be considered true art. A ballet that demonstrates nothing more than craftsmanship in matching steps to the music is incomplete and lacks organic majesty. If the creator is unable to acknowledge this responsibility, then he fails in his mission.

Good dance connects with viewers. This is because dance is a primitive art that has roots in all societies. In dance, one does not have to educate one's ear as with music. One does not have to expand one's vocabulary as with literature. Nor does one have to become expert on the subtlety of shapes and colors as with painting. We can appreciate dance because we all tap our feet to a cadenced drumbeat and sway to a rhythmical melody. It is in our being. So when we go to the theater to see dance, we identify with what we are observing more easily than with most other theater arts. However, the eye is more easily fooled by poor dancing. This is because even deficient choreographic endeavors are usually much better than what viewers are capable of creating themselves. Therefore, we tend to attempt appreciation of even undeserved mediocre efforts.

Most viewers are unable to identify the reasons for feeling unfulfilled as they watch a poor performance. It is likely that their uneasiness will only manifest itself as boredom. This can happen when a bad ballet is danced well, just as when a good ballet is poorly danced. And both can suffer when the music is inappropriate or poorly played. The three-part marriage of music, choreographic imagination, and movement must not be found lacking in any area, or else the whole endeavor suffers. In this respect, classical ballet is unique because it is a fusion of three arts—four, if acting is also included.

In recent years, due to the dearth of newly created masterworks, we have seen the attempted emergence of numerous new ballet choreographers. However, none has produced a memorable work for the ages. With few exceptions this has been going on for nearly a half century with little improvement. Instead, innovation has become the rule.

"Create something unique" is the mantra. "Startle the public—even shock audiences." If all else fails, then redo an established classic by putting a modern face on it. At least the music has already been proved successful. However, has human imagination become so stagnant that creativity is completely stifled? What purpose do the dance arts serve today? And how do the servants of dance propose to apply its process in the modern theater? These critical questions should impel the thoughts and actions of all serious dance art creators, while keeping in mind that most of the best dance masterworks are fantasies of escape that allow viewers to flee from mundane realities, at least for a short time.

Art must not stand still. That is obvious. And advances in any art must take it to a new level—but never downward. If an art seems stagnated, then it is the fault of its creators and presenters, not audiences. New styles and experimentations are to be expected, but not at the expense of basic artistic principles. The creation of original works of art suggests that the creators infuse power into their work, which elevates the product to heretofore un-attainable heights. The work's revelations offer new interpretations and in-sights. This is what makes a work of art memorable.

Most classical ballets of past centuries involved escapist themes. That era was followed by the creation of abstract works that focused more on beating hearts and pulsing brains. Tudor, Massine, and Balanchine are a sampling of creators in the latter genre. In their works, gestures and pantomime were used sparingly only to suggest mood and emotion. To be successful, both dramatic and abstract ballets need to be able to reach the audience in mean-ingful ways, each with its own emphasis. However, it should be clear that a genuine appreciation of abstract ballet derives from a greater understanding of the intricacies of more easily appreciated story or dramatic ballets.

Most recent attempts at creating full-length story ballets have been efforts by choreographers thoroughly immersed in the abstract genre. This being the background of their personal stage experience, they tend to create complex plots that are filled with many emotional trials and tribulations. Not enough care is given to defining their subjects. Another mistake is to utilize young dancers who lack life experiences that can make emotions poignant and dra-matically realistic.

Full-length ballets are expensive to produce. And few companies are large enough to cast a major work, especially in the United States, where ballet is privately funded for the most part. Therefore, lacking sufficient funds and time to develop the work, such projects are rarely considered seriously by today's directors. It is easier and less expensive for directors to do works of their own or bring in works that have already been performed by other com-panies. No director wishes to see unhappy audiences leave the theater. After all, his job is at stake. Therefore, it is safer to choose works that have already been proven, even if they are only moderately successful.

Ask yourself as you exit a performance, "What is it that I remember?" If your recollection fixes on the dancers' technical feats, then something is wrong. Classical dance must not become a circus of adept tricksters that succeeding generations of young dancers try to emulate or outdo. Models worthy of emulation should be dancers capable of raising aspirations from the mundane to the lofty heights of artistry where everything is possible. Being capable of doing thirty-two double fouettés en tournant or leaping into a spinning double revoltade should not be the standard that dancers strive for, even though it may be fun for dancers to occasionally extend their technical boundaries and for audiences to be momentarily awed.

As with all arts, classical ballet should raise viewers' perceptions to new levels of human understanding. This means that the primary mission of choreography is to educate and entertain and at the same time uplift the audience, not merely to provide an avenue for self-expression for the creator. Hopefully, the marriage of music, atmospheric design (costumes and scenery), and beautiful movement will take viewers on a journey that provides a message of inspired optimism.

For the most part, abstract or plotless choreography is a vehicle of artistic self-expression for the choreographer. At the same time, abstract choreography limits the dancers from fully expressing their own feelings and emotions. Not being able to become engaged with the character of a role relegates artists to being little more than tools in the hands of the choreographer—the sculptor's clay, so to speak. This approach to dance may be very satisfying to the choreographer and even interesting to watch when created by a talented craftsman. However, it is not always gratifying for the dancer. And the audience may be confused or unsatisfied to some extent.

Being able to lose oneself in the persona of a character—becoming a different person onstage—is a very satisfying artistic experience. The dancer can fully express the emotions of his or her character, while allowing choreographic demands and technical challenges to become the foundation on which to base their characterizations. "Speaking" through clearly defined gestures and expressions, in addition to the patterns of steps, are evident in nearly all ballet masterworks. The best ballets in this category merge all of these ingredients artfully.

There is another level of the art of classical ballet choreography that takes a more sophisticated approach. Successful ballets in this category, such as Antony Tudor's *Lilac Garden,* imply feelings and mood through choreographic style and the music.

A third level of the dance arts is purely abstract. It is simply a merger of music and movement whereby the dancers become the music, as it were. There is no room in such works for pantomime, overt feelings, or individual mood. The atmosphere is indefinable and open to a multitude of interpretations. Choreographers in this category sometimes let their dancers provide their own motivation. However, abstract choreographers often don't require or even desire individuality or emotions from their dancers. They believe that such performing concepts get in the way of their intended choreographic imagery.

In this regard, Balanchine once told me that he viewed the choreographer's relationship to his dancers as a jockey sitting astride a thoroughbred racehorse that only responded to the pull of the reins, the whip, and the pressure of the rider's legs and feet against its body. He explained that he did not want the horse to do anything that he did not specifically direct it to do and that he was not interested in individual interpretation.

Abstract choreography can also be punishingly difficult on dancers' bodies, as choreographers sometimes manipulate familiar or radically different movements to achieve sought-after effects. Many dancers have had their careers prematurely cut short due to severe injuries caused by movements that seemed possible in the mind of the choreographer but were, in fact, physically overtaxing and even dangerous. During rehearsals abstract choreographers often ask their dancers, "Can you do this step?" or "Do you think that you could twist yourself like that?" in their search for a desired effect.

It is well known that many major ballet companies have a high index of injuries. There are frequent last-minute casting changes, with numerous soloists and principals on the disabled list. The reason? Much of today's contemporary repertory involves extremely fast eccentric movements that satisfy choreographers' ideas of abstract imagery. However, their ideas also often break traditional rules for safe dancing, such as not placing heels on the floor during jumps, dancing off balance, or fast direction changes during turns and jumps.

Young dancers' bodies have a high tolerance for extreme physical demands, but repeated abuse and advancing years eventually catch up with even the most gifted dancer. Meanwhile, the implied rule of company life is to not complain about injuries as long as they are not crippling. "Just shake it off" is the common attitude imposed by many directors that makes many young dancers feel that if they ask for time off to properly recover from injuries, they may lose an opportunity to dance a desired role, be passed over for promotion, or be viewed by the director or choreographer as a wimp.

Finally, losing oneself in a role lets the dancer focus on the overall performance instead of choreographic demands, and it also allows him to live the music within the character he is portraying. It is a privilege to dance Balanchine's *Theme and Variations,* but it is more artistically satisfying to dance *Giselle.*

CHAPTER 24

What Is Wrong with Ballet in America?

---

*The creation of art is achieved when
mundane perceptions are elevated and
technique gives way to truth.*

A. Sage

The art of classical ballet seems to be at a critical juncture even though there
are many good dancers around and a proliferation of performing organizations. At first glance this would seem to be a healthy situation. But something is amiss that urgently needs our attention. The evidence is implied due
to the curtailment of corporate and foundation funding. In addition, many
ballet companies are run by directors with little if any previous management
experience. The proliferation of apprentice and traineeship programs, which
are designed to provide undertrained no-pay or low-pay dancers for struggling companies, is an indication that our art needs an overhaul.

Rather than improving the quality of classical ballet in the West, the in-
vasion of foreign dancers that began with Nureyev, Makarova, and Baryshnikov has precipitated a steady decline in the quality of dance education in
the United States. And the more they come, the worse the situation gets.
This is perplexing, because elsewhere in the world, the state of classical dance
training has improved enormously. Witness the influx of "Latinos," especially
from Cuba, Spain, and Argentina.

It all began back in April 1959, when the Bolshoi Ballet Company made
its debut tour of the United States in New York City at the old Metropolitan
Opera House. At that time, the Sol Hurok booking agency was deluged by
ticket order requests. It was rumored that wealthy socialites were sending

blank checks to the Hurok office with instructions to buy tickets for every performance and just fill in the amount. The lines were longer than for a Broadway premiere, with people camping out overnight to save a place in line. People in the "business" (professional dancers, students, choreographers, and teachers) were largely unable to buy tickets.

At the time, I was assisting Simon Semenoff, a Hurok appointed translator, to recruit fifty extras for the Bolshoi performances of *Romeo and Juliet* and *Swan Lake*. Seeing the difficulty that dancers were having getting tickets, I prevailed on the Bolshoi ballet mistress, Tamara Nikitina, to help remedy the situation. She spoke with the artistic director, Leonid Lavrovsky, who arranged with the Met's management to offer a special dress rehearsal "performance" to which only ballet people were invited to attend at no charge.

During that unforgettable tour, New York audiences were treated to the likes of ballerinas Galina Ulanova, Maya Plisetskaya, Raissa Struchkova, Nina Timofeyeva, Marina Kondratieva, Ludmilla Bogomolova, Nina Chistova, and Maya Samakhvolova. Male principals included Yuri Zhdanov, Nicolai Fadeyechev, Boris Khokhlov, Alexander Lapauri, Gennadi Lediakh, Vladimir Levashev, Georgi Farmanyants, Yaroslav Sekh, Gleb Evdokimov, and Alexander Radunsky. In addition we saw the two teen phenoms, Vladimir Vasiliev and Ekaterina Maximova, before their rise to stardom. What was almost as stunning was that the company had left nearly half of their two hundred dancers back home in Moscow to carry on with their normal season of performances.

Seeing one incredible dancer after another, along with a full complement of soloists and a magnificent corps de ballet totaling nearly one hundred dancers, was a mind-blowing experience. For us dancers, it was both inspiring and depressing, because we realized that we would never be able to dance like them. Not that we lacked the talent, but our teachers were not capable of taking us to those dizzying technical and artistic heights.

Yes, there were several "name" teachers around, many of whom had prominent careers in important companies, including some from the fabulous Diaghilev Ballets Russes and the later splinter companies such as those formerly directed by René Blum and the Marquis de Cuevas. And there were a few excellent choreographers around. However, the Bolshoi Russians were far ahead of us in ballet pedagogy and were thus able to stage truly memorable performances and receive applause that literally shook the rafters.

Behind the scenes, some of the Bolshoi ballet masters and teachers visited New York schools. Their verdict was that "ballet instruction in America is primitive, about where we were pre-1930." They reported that America had no coordinated teacher-training program or methodology designed to develop and nurture talent, and that anyone could call themselves a ballet teacher without possessing any credentials whatsoever.

Sadly, fifty years later, we find ourselves in the same situation. We have not taken advantage of the golden gifts that fell into our laps. Those first Russian defectors, and the many outstanding foreign dancers who followed, do not seem to have made the slightest impression on the majority of dancers and teachers they came into contact with. No one questioned why they were so much better than we were. We merely stood in awe of their abilities, or worse yet, we resented their presence. How ironic!

And so today, our companies are filling up with talented and well-trained foreign dancers. Look at any roster of both large and small companies across the United States. Many of the principals and soloists are Russians or Cubans or Spanish or from other countries including Japan, China, and other former Soviet satellites. Why is this happening? The answer is simple. Nearly all of these dancers have one thing in common. Either directly, or indirectly, their training is influenced by Agrippina Vaganova, the influential Russian master teacher and pedagogue.

Vaganova's influence has taken the world of ballet pedagogy by storm. There are some who would try to deny it, but the proof is plain to see. Who are the most important dancers today? Whom do audiences rush to buy tickets to see? Where do many top dancers come from? Who are the dancers who dominate the awards ceremonies of most international ballet competitions? In most instances, a truthful response to these questions will ultimately lead respondents to the Vaganova syllabus, which is behind the "conspiracy." And if not a direct product of her methodology, the source will be a derivative of her training style, such as the Cuban school that graduates outstanding students nearly every year.

The Cuban National Ballet School, today directed by Ramona de Saá, is able to attract talented students willing to devote themselves heart and soul to their ballet studies. After providing the elementary years of study, satellite schools throughout the country feed their best talent to the National School in Havana. The Cuban system has several hundred students, and it is run

like a true academy that includes all aspects of academic and artistic training. The best graduates are invited to join the Ballet Nacional de Cuba, now
directed by Alicia Alonso. Others have to settle for less prestigious positions
in smaller dance organizations.

The Ballet Nacional has grown from its origins as a company of around
forty dancers, following the Revolution in 1959, to more than one hundred
today. Like the Bolshoi, when they tour abroad, they leave behind a contin-
gent of dancers to carry on at home.

Defections from the Cuban Ballet Company may draw disparaging attention to the many political problems that exist. However, new graduates
replenish the ranks of defectors in short order. In effect, defections are a sort
of attrition mechanism that accommodates new (and often better) graduates from the school. And another benefit is derived. The increasing fame of
Cuban dancers around the world tends to celebrate one of the successes of
the Revolution.

In the early 1960s, Soviet ballet masters went to Cuba to work with
the company and also to help the Cubans establish a national school. The
original faculty of the new school was enlisted from the company's roster
of soloists and principal dancers, who were trained to teach the Vaganova
methodology. As a soloist and ballet master of the company, I was one of the
new teachers who began teaching not only company dancers but also young
students who were mostly recruited from orphanages and working-class
families. On that original faculty was company principal dancer Margarita
de Saá, who is Ramona's twin sister and also my wife.

(Note: A documentary entitled *Mirror Dance,* created by producers Fran-
ces McElroy and María Rodríguez, was shown to American audiences on
national public television, PBS. It documents the parallel lives of the de Saá
sisters, even though separated by distance and politics since 1964. The award-
winning film has been shown internationally at numerous film festivals, including Havana.)

The first Cuban National Ballet School studios were constructed on the
golf course fairways of a former private country club. The school was named
Cubanacán. In the beginning, the curriculum was entirely Vaganova based,
and it remained that way until it evolved into the Cuban method of ballet
pedagogy that is used today throughout the country. Fernando Alonso, who

was at that time the artistic director of the Ballet Nacional, and Ramona de Saá were instrumental in creating the new Cuban method from the foundations of the original Vaganova syllabus.

In communist China the Vaganova syllabus was also used to form the new national ballet academies. The same was done throughout all of the republics and satellite states under Soviet influence. Today Vaganova-trained teachers have taken the syllabus to Japan, Korea, and Taiwan as well as many other locations. It is time for the United States to eschew "sour grapes" and acknowledge that the system is undeniably a proven success. What can we learn from it?

In Russia, ballet pedagogy is taught as a five-year study program. Graduates receive a certificate that is the equivalent of our master's degree. Every facet of teacher training is addressed and studied in the minutest detail, with all aspects of the eight-year study program carefully outlined and reasoned through. All teachers in Russia must have a diploma, either from GITIS, the arts education institute in Moscow, or from the Russian Academy of Ballet in St. Petersburg.

Methodologies such as Vaganova's, when applied correctly, produce great artists. That should be the goal of all pedagogues. Regrettably, it is common today to attend ballet performances where audiences expect to see only prodigious technique, such as many pirouettes, superhuman high jumps complicated by multiple turns, and incredibly complex and dangerous landings as well as "attitude"—you know, an expression that exudes haughty sexiness. Unfortunately, many viewers are disappointed if they do not see these aberrations (much like MTV). We are being fed a diet of technical bravura at the expense of artistic splendor.

This brings us back to the question, Where are the great choreographers? Once again—where are the Petipas, the Fokines, the Ashtons, the Mac-Millans, the Crankos, the Grigorovichs, the Tudors, and the Balanchines? Does the legacy of these great creators exist today only to stimulate poor imitators?

There seems to be a plethora of wannabes that have little to add to the art and who are only capable of ego-sating innovations or "new" re-creations of classics. They may enjoy their moment of fame. But if their works lack the precepts of true art, what will happen when these pretenders are gone? Do their creations contain survival ingredients? Great ballet classics live forever, much like a Beethoven symphony, or an *Aida,* or the *Mona Lisa.* Time will test the survival issue.

And so what is to become of classical ballet? Let those who are serious artists and teachers be determined to avoid the trap of catering to charlatans. They are not worthy of our support. The limelight will fade from them fast enough. Their true worth will be discerned in the end, and real talent will rise from their immolated ashes. In the end, art will prevail. We must have faith.

CHAPTER 25 *Ballet Camp*

Work and play are words used
to describe the same thing under
differing conditions.

Mark Twain

Children of all ages are especially fond of spending brief periods away from home during carefree summer months. Until a few years ago there were Boy Scout and Girl Scout camps. There were YMCA camps and church camps. There were summer camps for nearly every imaginable sport activity, craft activity, and even art activity. Ballet camps were no exception. Initially they were promoted by established dance organizations, each of which claimed to offer the "best" experience to applicants.

Then someone had the bright idea of calling these summer dance camps "intensives." The word had a serious ring to it. And it wasn't long before professional ballet organizations saw this as a potential gold mine. To many neophytes, the word *intensive* somehow implied that students who attended would receive better training than they could possibly receive at home.

When major ballet companies and schools began offering summer intensives, it became clear that these camps represented a source of much needed revenue. During the "off season" of slow dance activity, normal fund-raising activities were reduced to a trickle. Seeing this lucrative potential, pioneers of summer intensives became increasingly enamored with the idea of tapping into students' searches for exceptional training. After all, most of these camps were offered by well-known dance organizations and "name" personalities.

Until then, only a handful of students were selected to attend elite schools for legitimate summer programs such as the School of American Ballet in

New York City. It was perceived that auditioning for and being selected to attend a summer intensive meant that the student was being asked to join an elite club of future professional dancers.

Intensives have become a big business. We now see an annual circus of dozens of summer camp auditions that compete to attract students from all over the country. It has become so lucrative that some of these organizations conduct camps in multiple locations to accommodate the overflow of applicants. Each year hundreds of hopefuls audition and are invited to give large amounts of their money for the privilege of spending a few weeks away from home in dance camps.

When intensives are sponsored by well-known ballet organizations, there seems to be a near fever-pitch obsession to be selected as one of the privileged chosen. There is a perception that it is a great honor to attend one of these special camps. "Maybe someone will notice me and invite me to join their company, or maybe I'll be chosen to be an apprentice or a trainee." In fact, such an outcome is highly unlikely, except for a handful of exceptionally gifted students, who more than likely would be offered such positions anyway.

The truth is that many of these increasingly expensive camps offer little in the way of permanent long-term benefits, except to the sponsors. As far as advancing careers, most summer camps are of marginal value, and the negatives often outweigh the positives. For the most part, programs are not designed to help students make the transition to the professional ranks, even though many camps are connected to professional companies. Simply put, they are profitable schemes designed to attract potential talent to company schools and ultimately to create a pool of no-pay or low-pay dancers to fill in as needed. Thus has been born the relatively new genre of dancer called "apprentice."

Really good dancers don't have trouble finding work, and talented students who have received a thorough dance education should not be satisfied with traineeships. Most new-hire major company dancers come from small regional companies, where they have already served what might be called a sort of "apprenticeship" as entry-level corps members. These already experienced dancers are seeking opportunities to advance their careers in better companies.

The majority of schools and teachers are unable to provide professional-level training. Therefore, company directors accept not quite ready students into their organizations as "trainees" or "apprentices." These titles have become the new jargon that in reality denotes "advanced students." The problem is that the reason directors do not hire these students as company dancers, and offer them apprenticeships instead, is usually because they perceive technical and artistic inadequacies: The student-dancer does not use her turnout, and her feet sometimes don't point. Her extensions are low. She needs to lose weight. Her jumps and turns are inconsistent. She doesn't perform very well. And her pointe work is weak.

Once a trainee or apprentice exhibits any of these deficiencies, it is unlikely that the director will patiently wait for future improvement to warrant giving a full corps contract. It is always more difficult to see beyond the negatives once they are firmly implanted in mind. And, in time, there will inevitably arrive a new face with all of the required "equipment."

But why are schools not providing the necessary training? Might it be that there are far too many teachers who lack experience and teacher training? And might it also be that many schools are now focused on more lucrative moneymaking activities such as camps and competitions?

During its thirty-five years of existence, my school, the Pennsylvania Academy of Ballet, has graduated nearly seventy students directly into professional companies throughout the world. Several have won high honors in international and national competitions. We have never had a single student return from a summer intensive who demonstrated any significant improvement or a better understanding beyond what he already knew. Such a result would seem to belie the claims of organizations touting such activities.

During the few short weeks of a typical summer intensive, students must be evaluated by teachers unfamiliar to them in order to be properly placed in the program. This takes time because classes are generally overcrowded and there are many faces and bodies to inspect. The net result is that there is much time lost to standing around.

Even astute teachers cannot see the arms, legs, and feet of more than fifteen or sixteen students. And in classes of thirty, forty, or fifty students, it is unlikely that essential corrections can be given to each participant that could possibly lead to long-term improvement.

Also, the highlight of most summer intensives is usually a showcase performance where everyone participates, regardless of their ability. Typically, young students are taught and coached by professional dancers on summer leave from their companies who have little or no teacher training. In an attempt to impress students and visitors, they devote valuable class time to rehearsing these end-of-camp shows. In such situations it is common to see students being taught ballerina-level variations that are far beyond their capabilities, both technically and artistically.

Nevertheless, in spite of the above limitations, participating students often feel that they are somehow close to the professional world of dance, especially if the intensive is sponsored by a well-known professional company. "Maybe someone will notice me" is the typical mantra.

When camp is over, the students return home, filled with a false sense of where they really are in their quest to become professional dancers. They often feel bored when they resume their normal routine of classes with their regular teacher(s) and are surrounded by the same familiar faces in the classroom. The excitement is gone. And it is not uncommon for students to consider changing schools based on a distorted view of where they truly are in the spectrum of professional dance.

Unless a student's training at home is poor to begin with, they will have benefited little from summer ballet camp, other than to get away from home and share an activity they enjoy with newfound acquaintances. If having fun is the primary motive for participating, I see little downside. However, after such an experience, serious students should honestly answer the question, Am I a better dancer for the experience? If their answer is dubious, then who is the beneficiary of their attendance at such expensive intensives? The answer should be apparent.

I would recommend that students take time off from dancing in the summer. Nothing will be lost, I assure you. Go to the beach. Go camping. Visit a national park. Go swimming. Play Ping-Pong. Take the money saved and attend performances of the best dance concerts in the area, including an occasional trip to a major dancer venue such as Lincoln Center in New York or the Kennedy Center in Washington, D.C. See live performances of a Broadway show, a play, an opera. Read a book. Read two books.

Then, when you are itching to get back to tendus in the fall, psych yourself up for your return to class. Dive in with a renewed focus and determination. Establish specific goals and work hard to achieve them. Be demanding of yourself and expect results. This would be a productive summer.

CHAPTER 26 *The Legacy of Agrippina Vaganova and Her Influence on Russian Ballet*

She was an absolute genius. Of her three thousand students, twenty-five hundred would never have become dancers were it not for Vaganova.

Maya Plisetskaya

A book on teaching classical ballet would not be complete without giving credit to Agrippina Yakovlevna Vaganova (1879–1951), one of the most important and influential pedagogues in classical ballet history.

Vaganova's influence on classical ballet is incalculable. She was indeed a true pedagogue genius and one of the most important classical dance teachers of all time. Her right to this accolade is based on the indisputable fact that her ingenious teaching methods have produced some of the greatest dancers in modern ballet history, beginning in the late 1920s and continuing even after her death until the present day. Thousands of students personally trained by her and students of teachers that she trained became professional dancers.

For the past seventy-five years, tightly controlled societies like the former Soviet Union and its satellites have been able to attain extraordinarily high levels in the arts. In classical ballet, students from the state-run dance academies of the former Soviet Union have achieved amazing accomplishments. Nearly every year extraordinary graduates are ready to step into retiring artists' shoes. And following their model, other non-Soviet-sphere countries like China, Cuba, Japan, and South Korea have done the same in just a few decades. What is common with most of these achievements is that they all are closely linked to Vaganova's heritage in some respect.

The Maryinski Theater in St. Petersburg, Russia, first opened in 1860, becoming home to the ballet company in 1894. Possibly no other theater in the world can boast of so many great dancers having danced on its stage. The school's connection to the company and the theater is a storybook relationship.

The climax of each year's graduation is a special performance where new graduates compete for invitations to join the Kirov Ballet. Not all graduates are invited, and those who are not chosen must look elsewhere for employment. Although no doubt disappointing to them, it is probable that all graduates find positions somewhere.

For the last several years the school's director has been Altinai Asylmuratova, an outstanding former prima ballerina of the Kirov Company. Most of the faculty are former dancers and are also graduates of the Institute for Advanced Pedagogic Artistic Studies, better known under the acronym GITIS (Gosudarstveny Institut Teatralnovo Iskustva), in Moscow. Certification requires completing a five- to six-year course of study. As a side note, the terms Kirov School and Bolshoi School are incorrectly used. The school in St. Petersburg, originally named after Vaganova, is now known as the Russian Academy of Ballet. The school in Moscow is called the Moscow Academy of Dance. In addition, other former Soviet republics continue to sponsor and operate their own ballet academies and theaters independently of Russia.

During Soviet times there were no civic ballet organizations or private schools. All schools were state academies funded by the central government under the aegis of the Ministry of Culture. Since the demise of the Soviet Union, funding for all arts organizations is much more restricted. Today, foreign students may be invited to attend if they are able to meet the high standards and pay tuition fees for the privilege. In addition, there have been some changes incorporated into the curriculum, which now includes modern dance.

Russian schools now have a pre-ballet level of nine-year-old hopefuls who study fundamentals taken from the I Class syllabus. They also work on musicality, flexibility, and strengthening. It is generally known that students in this group, who are invited to enter the academy, will have a head start when they begin the I Class during the regular course of study at age ten.

By employing this strategy, the school accelerates some of the material, which allows it to incorporate aspects of the II Class material into the curriculum for the I Class, etc., throughout the first several years of study, until graduation from the VIII Class at age eighteen.

Year 2007 was the 265th anniversary of the school in St. Petersburg. It was originally founded and named the Imperial Ballet Academy in 1738. For many years after Vaganova's death in 1951, the school was named the Vaganova Ballet Academy. Under its new name, the Russian Academy of Ballet has approximately three hundred students between the ages of ten and eighteen. They receive their academic schooling as well as their entire dance training there.

A typical school day for an advanced student might last eight to ten hours, including rehearsals in the evening for future performances of either the ballet company or the opera. It is a busy six-day week. Students receive a two-week break during the New Year holidays and have the summer off. They do not attend summer "intensives" or ballet camps. In 2005 only three girls and six boys among the graduates were invited to join the Kirov Company.

Vaganova was born in 1879. She entered the Imperial Ballet Academy and graduated in 1897. After several years in the corps de ballet, she was elevated to the rank of soloist, dancing mainly secondary roles in the classics. The ballerinas during that era were Anna Pavlova, Tamara Karsavina, Olga Preobrajenska, and Mathilde Kshesinska. Vaganova danced for the Maryinski Ballet until her retirement in 1916 at the age of thirty-seven. According to the custom, she was promoted to the rank of ballerina so that she would receive a larger pension.

According to her diary, it was apparent that Vaganova was not a very happy dancer. She lacked a graceful physical appearance and danced with an emphasis on strong technique rather than the artistic qualities so admired by critics and the public. Throughout her career she felt somewhat cheated, and although she respected her teachers, she also blamed them for her deficiencies.

During her time, there were several teachers with good reputations, including the Legat brothers, Nicolai and Sergei, and Pavel Gerdt. These men were also outstanding former dancers who had been trained by advocates of the French School extending back from Marius Petipa, Christian Johansson, and August Bournonville all the way to Jean Georges Noverre in the early eighteenth century.

Another prominent teacher came to Russia from the Italian School. Enrico Cecchetti descended from the line of Carlo Blasis, and through him to the common connection, once again Jean Georges Noverre. Even though Noverre was the link, the teaching styles of these teachers in the Russian schools were quite different.

Vaganova set out to study each of their teaching styles in depth. Eventually she discovered that they all had certain deficiencies. Therefore, she felt that their methods were incomplete, which was why so many dancers were lacking in various aspects of their technique. She found that the French School emphasized softness and fluidity, while the Italian School focused more on angularity and virtuosity. There was an obvious rivalry between the advocates of each, with little if any information sharing. They simply ignored whatever the other method had to offer. Vaganova also noticed that only Cecchetti worked with a fixed lesson plan. The others just improvised.

Just after the Bolshevik Revolution, Vaganova taught at Akim Volynsky's private school in St. Petersburg, where she began to formulate her unique theories and teaching style. Volynsky was a noted balletomane and critic. She remained there between 1918 and 1921, years of great turmoil in Russia when numerous dancers defected, including those who left Russia to join Serge Diaghilev's Ballets Russes.

Vaganova then joined the faculty of the Maryinski School, renamed the Leningrad Choreographic Technikum after the Revolution. She danced for the last time in a farewell benefit performance in 1922 in which appeared two of her young pupils, Marina Semenova and Natalia Kamkova. After her graduation in 1925 at age seventeen, Semenova became known as the first prima ballerina of Soviet ballet. She astonished everyone with her virtuosity and wide range of movement. However, the credit was not given to Vaganova, who had been her only teacher. Semenova was just considered a phenomenon.

Over the next several years Vaganova continued working and evolving her theories, which were based on the best elements of both the French and Italian Schools. Her new theories evolved into what has become the Russian School today.

Other outstanding students included Olga Jordan and Galina Ulanova. They were followed in 1931 by Feya Balabina and Natalia Dudinskaya. All possessed the same qualities of grace, plasticity of arms, strong backs, aplomb (vertical stability), and an overall dominion of their technique without weaknesses. In 1934, Vaganova was appointed director of the school. By then she was turning out a steady stream of extraordinary dancers who were far superior to their peers.

This had never been accomplished before by any teacher during ballet's history. What a milestone! Her methods revolutionized ballet training, and not only for female dancers. She dramatically changed the perception of male dancing. Today, many of the greatest male dancers come directly from this tradition including Rudolf Nureyev and Mikhail Baryshnikov.

The new generation of Soviet choreographers rushed to use her dancers in their ballets whenever possible. Vaganova, in turn, influenced the style of many new choreographers, since her dancers had fewer limitations and were easier to work with.

Her goal was to bring the human body into a state of complete harmonious coordination of all its parts. She was eminently successful, as the Kirov Company soon became full of her graduates, who were far superior to those trained by other teachers. Later, after retirement, many of her students went on to outstanding careers as teachers.

In her later years, Vaganova only taught the final two years of her students' training. She also taught the "Class of Perfection," a special class reserved for exceptional dancers that was created to bring out and refine the ultimate talents that the chosen dancers were capable of. It was from this class that most of the soloists and principal dancers came from.

Vaganova's book, *Basic Principles of Classical Ballet*, was published in 1934. It has been translated into many languages and is still considered an important theory guide, although not a definitive teaching tool. By the time she wrote it, her methods had been exclusively adopted throughout the entire union of Soviet republics. At her own request, her method is kept up to date. She was constantly revising her own syllabus based on new discoveries, in order to keep abreast of new developments in classical dance.

The last group of outstanding dancers personally trained by Vaganova included Irina Kolpakova, a pure classicist who danced with great refinement and technical ease. Her fluid arms and steely strong back, her precise musicality, and her artistry are trademarks of Vaganova's personal touch. Today, Kolpakova is a coach at American Ballet Theatre. The school is fortunate to have such a great artist who can pass on the Vaganova legacy.

Today, if one looks closely at the training of many professional ballet dancers, one will often find a Vaganova influence lurking somewhere in their background. Under the tutelage of a knowledgeable teacher who understands the basic principles of the Vaganova system, if the student begins his studies with a good mind and body, success is almost guaranteed. The reason for this is because Vaganova was a genius in figuring out which movements contribute to achieving the highest levels of technical mastery. And she never lost sight of the importance of artistry in everything she taught. For example, one did not just do pirouettes for their own sake or execute a soaring leap just to make a "wow!" impression. For her, each movement, pose, and gesture had a reason and a clear relationship to the qualities of music and the choreographic intent. I suspect that she might be turning over in her grave as the ballet world today seems more interested in spectacular technicians than consummate artists.

To achieve her goal Vaganova insisted that every ninety-minute lesson should include a minimum of twenty minutes of jumping, including a variety of petite allegro, middle allegro, and grand allegro steps and combinations. She always taught that allegro was the essence of classical dance, and that lessons with minimal or inappropriate jumps are useless, even detrimental. Therefore, carefully observing the organization of the allegro section of a lesson is a proper test when evaluating a teacher's competence. In other words, a lesson consisting of a one-hour barre, a couple of center combinations, and two or three jumps is a sign of an incompetent teacher, regardless of how entertaining the class may be or how famous the teacher.

Another important feature of Vaganova's method is the rigorous planning of each year of instruction including the daily lessons that comprise the monthly outline of study. While adhering to the syllabus, she recognized that there is room for teacher discretion. Nevertheless, she provided guidelines for when and where each new technical ingredient was to be introduced in the syllabus and how to accomplish it.

Today, as before, the national schools of Russia hold end-of-year exams. Not only are the students examined, but teachers must also demonstrate that they have taken their classes to the level of achievement that has been predetermined by the methodology committee as appropriate for the year. If there are glaring deficiencies, then the teacher is held accountable.

Until the mid-1960s, the curriculum for all academic choreographic ballet schools in the Soviet Union was based on a nine-year syllabus that started with students nine years of age. They graduated when they were eighteen. Most of the material was taught during the first eight years. The IX Class, which only included a small amount of new material, was considered a consolidation year. During that final year the strict adherence of wearing uniforms was not enforced as before, and students were encouraged to develop their own personalities and stretch their technical limits. This gave company directors an opportunity to identify the artistic potential of possible new stars.

After it was decided to drop the IX Class—and for the next thirty or so years—Russian schools utilized an eight-year syllabus that essentially compressed the original nine-year syllabus into eight years, beginning with ten-year-olds. The graduating age (eighteen) did not change. However, some teachers felt that many graduates of this shortened program were not as well prepared for the professional stage as previous generations were.

The Soviets also tried out an experimental six-year program of ballet studies. It was implemented to accommodate older beginners who missed the auditions for ten-year-olds. This special program allowed exceptionally talented older students to begin their studies at age twelve or even thirteen. Because these students were more mature and physically stronger that the ten-year-olds, the work of the first six years (elementary and intermediate levels) of the eight-year program of studies was compressed into four years. Then the students were incorporated into the final two (advanced) years of study along with their peers.

Natalia Makarova was one of these students. In later interviews she explained that the accelerated program did not adequately prepare her and that she had to continue learning on the job after she joined the Kirov Ballet Company. Rudolf Nureyev had a similar experience. This special program was later suspended.

These events led the methodology committee to institute a pre-ballet program that was designed to jump-start beginners by identifying potential talent. The class covers the fundamentals of music and dance and also employs special exercises to prepare their bodies for the rigors of the I Class.

In the beginning the committee experimented with two pre-ballet levels, an X Class of eight-year-olds and a Class of nine-year-olds. Now a single pre-ballet class permits the original eight-year syllabus to accelerate the teaching of each year's material by a small degree. Essentially, what has happened is that the committee has effectively reverted back to a nine-year program of study that begins with nine-year-olds. As mentioned before, seniors of the VIII Class are still eighteen when they graduate.

The following is a brief summary of the current curriculum goals in Russia for each of the eight years of the study program for classical dance that begins with boys and girls who are ten years of age:

I Class. First are taught fundamental exercises for learning the basic stance, the positions of the body, the positions of the feet, use of the arms, head, and eyes, and the development of good habits for coordinating movement.

In the beginning, students learn most movements while facing the barre, holding with both hands. Most exercises are first taught to the side. Then, still facing the barre, they are taught backward. Finally, exercises are taught forward with one hand on the barre. Later, upon assimilation, students execute the same movements holding the barre with one hand while facing along the barre.

Arms are introduced as a preparation and as a conclusion for each exercise. Fundamentals of turnout are taught. After assimilation, many barre exercises are introduced in the center exercise. All allegro jumps and pointe exercises are introduced facing the barre, holding with both hands. Later they are brought to the center.

II Class. Exercises from the first year are reviewed, adding more repetitions and faster tempos. Emphasize developing strength in the legs and feet through the use of demi-pointe and pointe. Also, greater emphasis is placed on the coordination of the arms in preparations and conclusions of exercises.

Épaulement is introduced in the center and later at the barre. At first, movements are executed en face. Then the same movements are done alternating with épaulement. Music accompaniment can be more varied as to rhythm and tempo. Students learn when to use the different heights of the working leg (22½, 45, and 90 degrees).

III Class. Consolidate all of the previous elementary material. Emphasize the clarity of execution; more use of demi-pointe at the barre and in the center; learning elementary turning movements including turns on two legs and pirouettes; acceleration of tempos; and more use of large and small poses and épaulement. At the conclusion of some barre exercises, students hold balances on demi-pointe on both legs or on one leg before returning to fifth position (while removing the hand from the barre). Balancing positions may be sur le cou-de-pied or using extensions of the working leg. Exercises are done with épaulement and all directions and poses. Beats are introduced in simple jumps.

IV Class. Increase complications including exercises with half turns on one leg; more steps complicated with beats; tours en l'air for the boys; promenades (tours lents) in big poses; and preparations with two pirouettes.

V Class. Work on more complex beats; pirouettes with preparations from various poses and positions; more complex transitions from one pose to another; development of plasticity (supple controlled strength); first attempts at developing elevation in big jumps; tours fouettés on pointe for girls (four turns).

VI Class. Study jumps with a variety of more complex preparations; development of ballon in the big jumps; and more complex beats at faster tempos. Incorporate two pirouettes in barre exercises, and tours fouettés on pointe for girls (eight turns).

VII Class. Polish the material from previous years (mastery). Accelerate tempos. Include big jumps in isolation in longer and more strenuous adagios. Begin double pirouettes in big poses. Pointe combinations are constructed in a more dancerly fashion (mini variations). Excerpts from classical ballets can be taught in pointe lessons. Practice tours fouettés on pointe for girls (sixteen turns).

VIII Class. Work on mastery of all movement from previous years. Emphasize artistic qualities in preparation for the stage; use of more lengthy and complex adagio combinations; longer and more strenuous allegro combinations. There is a special emphasis on virtuosity and artistry with gifted students. Work on grand pirouettes à la seconde (boys class), and tours fouettés on pointe for girls (thirty-two turns).

Main features of the Vaganova method are:

1. Rigorous planning of the entire lesson.
2. Complexity of exercises that are directed at creating well-rounded virtuoso technique.

3. Insistence on mastery of each step, including every detail of épaulement and port de bras.

4. A conscious rather than a rote approach to learning. Pupils are expected to be able to explain each step, including the reasons for the unsuccessful as well as the successful execution of steps.

5. Emphasis on training the trunk of the body (the basic stance) as evidenced by a strong back. Vaganova believed that a well-developed trunk was a major prerequisite to overall body control.

6. Development of aplomb (vertical stability), which is the foundation for controlling multiple turns and complicated jumps.

7. The importance of allegro (the dynamics of jumping), including a powerful takeoff and a soaring quality during flight.

8. Fluidity and plasticity of the arms and upper body.

9. A noble carriage of the head and eyes.

10. Attention to details.

Vaganova turned the daily grind into artistic endeavor. Her students did not simply copy their teacher. They learned why they were supposed to dance a certain way and no other. She was interested in the needs of her students and what was necessary for them to achieve higher technical and artistic success. These are the "secrets" of her system.

We should count ourselves most fortunate to be able to benefit from Vaganova's lifelong dedication to the art of classical dance.

Appendix

Bits and Pieces

I do not expect all of the following "bits and pieces" to be groundbreaking or unique revelations. They are meant to be bulletlike reminders. No doubt, some have already been touched on in other sections of this book, while others may have been mentioned in my previous book, *Teaching Classical Ballet*. Some are indeed more than mere "bits" or "pieces" and could very likely stimulate further research that may well provide additional revelations for serious students of the art of classical ballet.

Please remember that when repetitions are encountered, they appear because I consider them important enough to reiterate, and I wish to impress their significance upon patient readers. Do not dismiss ideas that you initially disagree with. You may later find that they have relevance in your work, or you may grow to a deeper understanding of teaching principles. The following bits and pieces have been proven to lend significant aid in refining teaching concepts and are therefore pertinent. They are in random order, and there is no implied ranking of importance.

1. Teachers should not abandon the traditions of proven past masters when formulating their own methods. The fundamental artistic aims of classical ballet have remained constant since its creation. While there have been technical advances through the years, creativity during the lesson should be the teachers' primary concern so that realistic goals can be achieved.

2. Classical ballet is a child born of and for the theater. The primary object is to influence the viewer with expressive actions and meaningful gestures that are pure and uncluttered.

3. Students of classical dance must be taught that technique is the apparatus that facilitates the expression of thoughts and feelings. Technique

is not merely refined or spectacular movement, even at the highest levels of achievement. Its main function is to free dance artists from physical limitations so that their art can shine through.

4. To achieve high goals you must be uncompromising in your belief that you are on the right path and that you will succeed.

5. Spring into jumps (and relevés) from the heels pushing against the floor. This requires a proper distribution of weight and correct placement.

6. A good jumper always feels in balance—and looks like it, too.

7. During jumps there must be a harmonious coordination of the arms and legs, so that they help each other. This is not only physically necessary but also visually important.

8. Distinguish between "connected" and "disconnected" movements of arms and legs in jumping. Both are needed.

9. Connected movements aid in providing maximum elevation to jumps, where all ingredients, working together, contribute.

10. Disconnected movements teach isolation while maintaining complete control, so that there are no involuntary reactions.

11. Dancers must develop mental toughness—a commitment to do whatever is required to accomplish the movement. For example, pull up working leg muscles and straighten joints completely before transferring weight from one leg onto the other when executing a jeté onto demi-pointe to a big pose; or stay in balance for a moment after a pirouette is completed, before coming down from demi-pointe; or do an entire exercise in the center on demi-pointe.

12. Dancers must be just as pulled up at the bottom of a plié as they are when trying to balance on demi-pointe or while jumping.

13. Much of what teachers must do to achieve results with their students is to make them confront seemingly impossible tasks (for them at that particular stage of their development).

14. Students rarely know what is best for them. This includes professional dancers who often mistakenly begin to work slower and slower in class as they age. Every dancer needs a second pair of eyes to "see" what is needed.

15. An oxymoron? Students must be taught how to resist certain movements while at the same time letting them happen (for example, raising the leg to a high extension while maintaining the imperatives of the basic

stance). This is taught by practicing the movements very slowly in the beginning (relevé lent, développé, fondu, rond de jambe, etc.).

16. Make sure that the imperative ingredient for each jump is thoroughly understood. (Is it a traveling step? Or a high leap demanding elevation?) For example, sissonne fermé is primarily a vertical jump that also travels, whereas grand jeté is primarily a traveling step that also jumps up.

17. When students reach the middle to upper intermediate level of technical development, they should be challenged repeatedly. At first, these challenges might seem impossible. Some students might even resent such impositions of difficulties. But it is imperative to persist. As they begin to overcome the difficulties, little by little, the students will no longer dread what teachers throw at them. In fact, they will begin to look forward to new challenges. Once overcome, these become milestones. Examples are basic exercises that are complicated by adding turns or are done entirely on demi-pointe.

18. Teachers must develop the ability to devise exercises that make sense and fit together logically, including adequate time for preparations, shifting balances from one leg to the other, changes of direction, and clean endings. Combinations that look and feel awkward or uncomfortable are signs of a poor teacher. Well-developed (planned) lessons always make sense. The exercises should also lead to a predetermined goal for the day's lesson. Otherwise, you are just filling up time with a hodgepodge of disjointed movements. The structure of logical movement design is also the keystone of good choreography.

19. Although a desirable goal, feeling good while performing doesn't always translate into looking good. It is always better to look good, whether the viewer is an unsophisticated audience member or a master teacher. Feeling bad may just be the result of trying to break bad habits that might feel good but need to be gotten rid of.

20. Teachers' exercises must not be predictable. Inject surprises such as movements that travel upstage or momentarily face upstage diagonals. Use uneven numbers of repetitions (3s, 5s, 7s) or split phrases (two reps of a step that ends a phrase followed by two more reps of the same step that begins a continuing new phrase). Repeat a step at double time (two changements in 1/4 notes followed by three changements in 1/8 notes).

21. Good teachers design exercises that can logically be reversed.

22. After the barre exercise, place students in precise rows in the center so that students in the second row stand between the students in the front row (one student in each space, checkerboard fashion). Place students in their assigned rows randomly, so that students will not know where they will be standing until you assign positions. Make each day's row assignments completely random to avoid the appearance of favoritism. Pay attention to everybody, no matter where they are standing.

23. Be clear about how some movements can be done as steps themselves and also as preparations for other steps (chassé, pas de bourrée, pas couru, sissonne tombé, glissade, assemblé, etc.).

24. Ballet technique is a means for expressing ideas and emotions. The ideas must always be clear, and they must not be boring. The dancer/actor must constantly search for ways to express ideas and emotions that can be understood by the audience. This often requires the performer to lose himself in his role and become the persona he is portraying, and he must be able to convince the viewer of the truth of his portrayal. These are ingredients of the Stanislavski method of acting and are well worth studying. Read books by Konstantin Stanislavski.

25. What makes dance boring?

   A. Poor dancing.
   B. Poor choreography that doesn't give the dancer an opportunity to express himself.
   C. Inappropriate music, movement, costumes, scenery.
   D. An artistic interpretation that is confusing or inaccurate.
   E. Unfocused eyes and lack of expression.

Begin to instruct your students about the importance of these stagecraft concepts early.

26. Our objective as ballet teachers, indeed as all educators, should be to extract the highest possible results from the material placed in our care; to lead our students to discover qualities they possess but are unaware of; to awaken dormant possibilities; and to encourage students to put forth their strongest efforts to free themselves from limitations, both mental and physical.

27. A good teacher enjoys his work and helps his students enjoy their ef-

forts. A great teacher loves his work and freely and passionately uses all his experience and knowledge to help his students find their highest potential.

28. The mundane has no place in the ballet classroom, which should be a magical place of the theater where all things are possible.

29. Anyone can claim the title of "ballet teacher." Indeed, everyone who teaches ballet does so. But few (if any) can rightfully claim the title of "master teacher." If you aspire to that supreme level of recognition, you must study, work consistently, and avoid complacency at all costs. True pedagogy demands that one never be satisfied with mediocrity, neither in your students or in yourself. Be worthy of your calling.

30. The great baseball center fielder, Joe DiMaggio, was once asked how he kept striving for excellence when he had already attained fame. He said, "There is always some kid who may be seeing me for the first time or for the last time. I owe him my best."

31. Finished dancers always include in their execution of classroom exercises a theatrical ingredient that transcends the academic. On the other hand, most students, regardless of their talent and technical ability, let the struggle become too obvious, which affects the overall appearance of what they are doing. Students tend to allow their efforts to become more important to them than the artistic expression that makes the movement beautiful.

32. Responding to an admirer's compliment, the painter Winslow Homer said, "What they call talent is nothing but the capacity for doing continuous hard work in the right way."

33. Pursue excellence! Speaking to graduates of MIT at Cambridge in 2003, former senator George Mitchell said, "The education you've received at this great institution is important, even necessary, but it is not a guarantee of self-worth. It is not a substitute for a life of effort. How you do it is important, just as important as what you do. If you take pride in what you do, you will excel."

34. The ballet teacher's goal should be to instill in his students seriousness and respect for what they are doing and the understanding that dancing is a privilege and a discipline deserving work.

35. "Ballet Theory of Relativity"—Rehearse for one minute in pointe shoes with tired, blistered feet, and it seems like an hour. Dance for an hour an important role for a gala performance with the same tired, blistered feet, and it seems like a minute.

36. There are many exercises in a well-constructed technique class that strengthen the feet for pointe work. However, if you do a great number of pliés, tendus, ronds de jambes à terre, and développés in pointe shoes, you are not developing pointe work. You are only wearing the shoes.

37. An observation of American dancers in the Prix de Lausanne competition from 1999—All of the Americans dancers were eliminated during the trials exhibiting the same basic faults: a lack of correct port de bras; difficulty executing fast beats; no understanding of épaulement including head positions; their exercises began and ended sloppily; and their expressions showed a lack of confidence. After they were eliminated, the Americans and their coaches claimed favoritism from the judges who selected, for the most part, graduates from well-known national ballet academies. The Americans were clearly discouraged by the competition and felt discriminated against. However, it must be said that they and their teachers should learn from this experience and shape up. Unfortunately, not much has changed since then.

38. Although a modern dance icon, Martha Graham left numerous insights that are apropos to ballet dancers. She said that dancers learn their craft and master their instrument, the body, in the studio, where they also cultivate an awareness of the head, arms, torso, and legs. They learn flexibility and strength so that they can turn and leap with control. She reminded us that dancers must be realistic. Either the foot is pointed, or it is not. Dreaming will not point it for you. These astute admonitions apply to every aspect of learning how to dance. The above observations require discipline and conscientiousness. It is not the mere repetition of steps that achieves excellence. It is an absolute inner necessity that is imposed upon yourself. The final goal is freedom from limitations, not just freedom to perform phenomenal physical feats, but to convincingly express spontaneity and simplicity even after performing the same role for years. This requires discipline imposed from within, upon yourself. Just to go out on the stage and throw yourself about is not art. You can feel like an angel. But if you have no vocabulary or discipline, you can fall flat on your face—and you would deserve to.

39. Art is not a pastime to be played with. True art has deep human meaning. It should be respected because it reveals the inner spirit of what humanity is capable of. Art is not for everybody. It is an elite activity. Few are born gifted. Even fewer have the conscientiousness and discipline to work their talents to a level of true art.

40. Talent in ballet is not a beautifully pointed foot, or a long elegantly sculptured leg, or high turned out extensions. These are only tools—necessary perhaps, but only tools. True talent combines these necessary tools with unique abilities and powers that elevate observers to a higher level of aesthetic consciousness.

41. If the art of dance is to be raised to the same sublime level of music (especially music composition), then there must be no compromise in the effort to elevate the artistic standard. Mediocrity must never be tolerated.

42. A common characteristic of ballet study in the United States is to advance students too quickly without their mastering the essential components that comprise the steps. Without a solid foundation, slipshod execution is likely and injury is possible.

43. There is no justification for adopting practices in our work merely because they are popular or are being used elsewhere by "name" advocates. Search for the true precepts of knowledge even if it means that you must stand alone. Your students' accomplishments will justify your methods.

44. Regarding the current trend toward modern views of classical ballet—it is easier to change the choreography of an established ballet classic than it is to choreograph an original new ballet worthy of a place in ballet history that matches the quality of the great masterpieces.

45. Advice to students preparing to audition:

A. Do not wear layers of clothing. Directors want to see your body. Get used to this by wearing only a leotard and tights in class. No warmers.
B. Follow instructions. Do exactly what you are told. Pay attention to details.
C. Sometimes during auditions, directors will give a correction just to see how well you take it and apply it.
D. Always try to position yourself in the front of the group you are placed in.
E. Perform! Even if it is just a simple tendu exercise.

46. It is not politically correct to say it, but weight is a big issue with most dance jobs. Directors will not hire dancers who are overweight. If dancers have a weight problem, they must work on it before they audition. But they must be sensible and thoughtful about how they go about it. This advice may not be what dancers want to hear, but it is the truth.

47. Good teachers have to be good salesmen. If you can't sell, you can't teach.

48. Teachers have to be risk-takers. You have to stick your neck out.

49. Teachers must tell their students when they do well. However, teachers must be tough, and compliments should not be mere flattery or ego-boosters. There has to be a basis of truth. Teachers must also tell their students that they can do well, even while telling them that they are not yet succeeding.

50. Good teachers get involved in the lives of their students, not as meddlers but as interested parties. However, even when criticized, students must know that their teachers respect and love them as individuals and also believe in them.

51. Dwelling on the negative only contributes to its power.

52. The difference between sport and art: sport requires you to give yourself to the goal of winning; art demands that you give yourself to the process of creativity.

53. At all costs, avoid the three ugly *T*'s: Trivial, Trite, and Tedious.

54. Give special emphasis to the study of épaulement. It colors and enriches fundamentals. Port de bras and gestures in the art of ballet have a dual purpose. They contribute to the completion of technical tasks and also add meaning to movement. Just as an expressive face gives clarity to emotion, the hands and arms contribute artistic eloquence to poses and movements.

55. Being exposed to many schools of pedagogy often inhibits the acquisition of true knowledge. Mixing ideas imposes confusion, even if each method is capable of achieving positive results. Students should never be placed in the untenable position of deciding which theory is the best, especially when ideas conflict.

56. Pirouettes should be considered turning relevés. The spin, provided primarily by a well-connected torso, should begin immediately as the relevé begins. The rotating body must turn as a collected and coordinated entity, not as a gathering of parts.

57. Always maintain the building block foundation of the basic stance in all things—no twisting and no leaning. This is sometimes anatomically impossible. But never tell the students that this is so. They must work hard at maintaining TBS in everything they do.

58. When executing arabesque and attitude poses, the knee of the working leg must be directly behind the back in the area between the corresponding

shoulder and hip. Exactly how high will depend on the individual dancer's extension capabilities and the desired aesthetics of the given pose.

59. Watch the top of the head of students as they attempt to relevé or jeté (piqué) into arabesque and attitude poses. If the head appears to drop down or jut forward, the movement is being done incorrectly. These poses are supposed to give the impression of being poised for flight, and the head should therefore rise to the final pose.

60. Every grand allegro step, to be optimally executed, requires a perfectly balanced takeoff moment to efficiently use all vertical impelling forces that must collaborate to propel the body upward—around—forward—backward—or sideways (in whatever configuration or combination), in order to maximize the effectiveness of the leap and give the strongest impression to the viewer.

For example, when executing grand jeté, the leading leg must continue to extend and lead the body forward, even after arriving at the apex of the jump and into the landing. The perfect grand jeté should illustrate the image of a dancer sailing through the air in an upside-down Y position. This means that the body is vertical, while the legs are open and extending forward and backward at equivalent heights. This position must be reached no later than the apex of the jump and held as long as possible. It begins with a balanced deep plié on the supporting leg, followed by an explosive takeoff combined with a coordinated use of legs, arms, and upper body, which all add propulsion and trajectory. (Note: The study of all grand allegro steps and of many mid-allegro jumps requires a similar analysis.)

61. Ask yourself, "Am I really thinking? Or am I just rearranging prejudices?"

62. All teachers and serious artists must repeat the following mantra ten times (maybe even a hundred times): "In art nothing should ever happen accidentally."

63. It is imperative to search for ways to color your dancing, whether it is by adding individual subtle nuances to a simple combination or expressing the spirit of a character you are portraying. Penetrate the superficial to bring out deeper meaning.

64. Never let the impossibility of achieving perfection prevent you from striving for excellence. In this struggle, students must be taught that mistakes are okay as they reach for higher goals.

65. Turn off the voice in your head that tries to convince you that you can't do something.

66. It is up to you to take the appropriate steps to create a fulfilling and flourishing life. It is up to you whether or not to focus on what makes you miserable. Get into the habit of focusing on the joy of dancing, teaching, living, etc., not on how difficult it is.

67. In class every exercise should be an exhibition of perfectly executed classical technique combined with a liberal dose of individual artistry.

68. Most truly great artists are not vain creatures. They just believe in striving for perfection, and they are good at it. They see the challenge of the task at hand and deal with it. They do not brag of their successes or accomplishments. They don't need to. Their work speaks for itself. They do not see humility as a weakness. Only the truly great are that simple.

69. In the arts it is important to pay attention to trifles. Nothing is as important as trifles properly integrated at the right time.

70. Music composers use instruments to hear their finished compositions. However, in their minds the melody is perfect. Likewise, choreographers envision perfect dance patterns and rightfully expect their dancers to re-create them perfectly. Students must learn this professional imperative by rising to the challenge of re-creating the teacher's image of perfectly executed combinations.

71. The pathway of progress is paved with discipline. Learning something new or improving on what you already know is sometimes frustrating. The struggle to reach new plateaus can be daunting. Nevertheless, it is the true artist's mandate.

72. Discipline and conscientiousness applied in the right way can lead to milestones of achievements. The key to success in this struggle is uncovering "the right way."

73. How does one discover the right way? By discerning which path (method or theory) has a consistently proven track record. Be skeptical of enticing theories that emanate from the lips of articulate so-called masters. Demand proof.

74. There is always a best way to proceed, even though it is a commonly held belief that there are many valid ways to climb the mountain. Other ways may eventually lead to some measure of achievement, but the cost may be frustratingly slow progress.

75. Most great artists, during their formative years, unreservedly put themselves into the hands of trusted teachers who were able to guide them to mastery.

76. Enlightened students put aside ego, pride, and self-importance, which are impediments to progress. They attain their goals by running the race with single-minded purpose.

77. It is more comfortable to continue working with what is familiar—at levels already achieved—than to step up and confront new challenges and the possibility of failure. However, this confrontation is the only way to overcome self-doubt. The step-by-step climb, liberally strewn with small successes, proves to the disciplined worker that goals can be realistically achieved, and no task will ever seem unattainable. Therefore, every challenge becomes an opportunity to prove the worth of previous levels of achievement. Even goals that appear out of reach will not seem unattainable, because previous goals that once seemed impossible will have been attained.

78. Do not get caught up in the fever of seeking out teachers who tout new methodologies that have no foundation other than to be innovative. In the final analysis, all correct classical ballet teaching methods are based on similar principles. The best teachers are those who demonstrate a proven command of these principles, not those who mesmerize novices with clever-sounding words.

79. Avoid mediocrity at all costs. It is self-perpetuating.

80. The main function of most small regional ballet companies is to provide work and an artistic outlet for dancers, directors, and choreographers who are unable to obtain positions in major companies.

81. Dancing at the professional level is a performing art. At the same time, it is show business. Ballet companies do not exist to satisfy dancers', choreographers', and directors' egos. Their mandate comes from expectant audiences who pay dearly to experience the highest possible quality of art. This unselfish outlook must be the guiding principle of dedicated artists.

82. The ideal ballet student (in addition to possessing requisite physical gifts):

    A. Is intelligent, conscientious, focused, disciplined, and hardworking.

    B. Thrives on challenges.

    C. Has an acute sensitivity and feeling for music.

    D. Is aware that classical ballet is art, not activity.

E. Has the positive attitude that the glass is always half full, not half empty.

F. Understands that career-track preparations have little to do with dance camps, traineeships, and a variety of teachers.

G. Knows that setbacks are just temporary.

H. Listens to and applies every correction.

I. Leaves all mundane distractions out of the studio during class time.

83. A paradox: One learns more about dancing after learning how to teach.

84. Inexperienced dancers, even talented ones, often try to impress their audiences through the size and quantity of their dancing rather than by the quality of their art. This is also a common shortcoming of students.

85. Dancing a combination (variation) must build to a crescendo that ends on an "up" note. Otherwise, the viewer feels let down.

86. Teachers should learn how to devise combinations that can be executed on both sides and in the reverse.

87. Each lesson should have a unique purpose, leitmotif, or plan.

88. Each exercise combination has its own value: for example, warm-up, stretching, quick attack, muscular development (strength), stamina, soaring qualities during big jumps, etc.

89. It is illogical to invent combinations just to be different or to impose challenges beyond the students' ability to cope. Overly simple combinations are equally undesirable.

90. When teaching combined classes for both female and male students, it should be remembered that combinations (especially in the center and allegro sections of the lesson) sometimes demand different emphasis from the opposite sexes. For example, boys do not learn piqué turns, pas de chats, or pas courus, and girls do not learn double tours en l'air, cabrioles in big poses, and certain other virtuoso steps usually reserved for male dancers. Teachers should research this matter so they don't emphasize steps for their students inappropriately. Also, boys should be taught to execute certain steps in a more resolute and virile manner, whereas the girls should perform the same steps in a somewhat softer and prettier fashion.

91. Students need rest. Their muscles and minds need repose to recover from the demands of daily lessons. There is nothing wrong with taking time

off. Teachers should not encourage their students to take classes seven days a week or to take three or four classes per day or to go from one summer "intensive" to another. Fatigue from overly demanding schedules often leads to injuries that require medical attention and enforced rest. After winter and summer sessions end, students should take a break, visit relatives, go to the beach, ride bikes, go swimming, learn how to cook, knit a sweater.

92. The great twentieth-century Soviet teacher Asaf Messerer, after an illustrious career as a virtuoso dancer with the Bolshoi Ballet, passed his wisdom on to hundreds of students, many of whom were leading dancers of the company. While basing his methods on past masters, Messerer devised the following system for constructing lessons for the week. Each day had a theme based on allegro steps.

> A. Monday—Assemblé
> B. Tuesday—Sissonne
> C. Wednesday—Cabriole
> D. Thursday—Jeté
> E. Friday—Pas de basque, saut de basque, pas ciseaux, etc.
> F. Saturday—Combinations of all of the above.

93. Teachers must try to stimulate passion in their students. It often brings out latent talent.

94. Talent in classical ballet is the ability to take a strict academic movement and turn it into a work of art, where the technique disappears and only the qualities of dance are visible.

95. Complacency and boredom are the mortal enemies of teachers.

96. The profession of teaching is far more onerous than that of dancing. Dancers only have to answer to themselves. Teachers must answer to all of their students.

97. Teachers must convey a fascination of the art to their students.

98. A call to ballet company directors: Set high standards! Don't be satisfied with anything less than the best! Compromises only serve to lessen the quality and excellence that your audiences deserve!

99. The major difference between most students and top professionals: Students only work hard enough to improve; professionals work until they make no mistakes.

100. Most professional dancers need to dance. They have gone beyond

just liking it. They would feel unfulfilled if they could not dance. They might complain about trivialities, but they love what they are doing and would not do anything else.

101. All good dancers are risk-takers. They are not cautious, hesitant, or doubtful. Such attributes describe a boring dancer. It is okay to make mistakes, but one must never be boring!

102. Dance is a show business calling that demands total commitment to giving the audience a thrilling theatrical experience.

103. If you have chosen to pursue ballet as a career, not only must you love the work but you must also love the process. It should be an exciting and unforgettable ride.

Procrastination

By A. Sage

At twenty, man lives in ignorant bliss,
dancing to pride's pale tune.
At thirty, he suspects himself a fool;
Knows it at forty and reforms his plan.
At fifty, he rues his delay
and resolves to press his prudent purpose.
At sixty—seventy—eighty . . .
Alas, no time.

Suggested Reading

Blasis, Carlo. *An Elementary Treatise upon the Theory and Practice of the Art of Dancing*. Translated by Mary Stewart Evans. New York: Kamin Dance Gallery, 1900, 1944; reprint, New York: Dover, 1968.

Dolin, Anton. *Pas de Deux: The Art of Partnering*. With an introduction by Arnold Haskell. New York: Kamin Dance, 1949; reprint, Mineola, N.Y.: Dover, 2005.

Grant, Gail. *Technical Manual and Dictionary of Classical Ballet*. 3rd ed. New York: Dover, 1982.

Kostrovitskaya, Vera. *101 Classical Dance Lessons from the First through the Eighth Year of Study with Forty-eight Lessons on Pointe*. Translated by John Barker. New York: Barker School of Classical Ballet, 1979.

Kostrovitskaya, Vera, and Alexei Pisarev. *School of Classical Dance*. Translated by John Barker. Moscow: Progress, 1978.

Krasovskaya, Vera. *Vaganova: A Dance Journey from Petersburg to Leningrad*. Translated by Vera M. Siegel. Foreword by Lynn Garafola. Gainesville: University Press of Florida, 2005.

Roslavleva, Natalia. *Era of the Russian Ballet*. Foreword by Ninette de Valois. New York: Dutton, 1966.

Serebrennikov, Nikolai. *Pas de Deux: A Textbook on Partnering*. 2nd ed. Edited by Marian Horosko. Translated by Elizabeth Kraft. With added material translated by Sergey Goordeev. Gainesville: University Press of Florida, 2000.

Stanislavski, Konstantin. *My Life in Art*. Translated by J. J. Robbins. New York: Meridian Books, 1956.

Tarasov, Nikolai I. *Ballet Technique for the Male Dancer*. Adapted by Marian Horosko. Translated by Elizabeth Kraft. Edited by N. M. Vovnoboy. Garden City, N.Y.: Doubleday, 1985.

Vaganova, Agrippina. *Basic Principles of Classical Ballet*. 2nd English ed. Translated by Anatole Chujoy. Incorporating all the material from the 4th Russian ed. Including Vaganova's sample lesson with musical accompaniment, translated by John Barker. New York: Dover, 1969.

White, John. *Teaching Classical Ballet*. Gainesville: University Press of Florida, 1996.

JOHN WHITE is the author of *Teaching Classical Ballet* (UPF, 1996) and is codirector of the Pennsylvania Academy of Ballet. He was a soloist and maitre de ballet of the Ballet Nacional de Cuba and the head instructor and interim ballet master of the Pennsylvania Ballet Company. Since 1980, he has conducted seminars for dance teachers based upon the Vaganova method, training nearly eight hundred teachers from all over the world.